What's Doin' the Bloomin'?

What's Doin' the Bloomin'?

A Pictorial Field Guide of Wildflowers,
by Season, of the Upper Great Lakes Regions,
Eastern Canada and Northeastern U. S. A.

Text and photography by
Clayton & Michele Oslund

Printed by:
    Corporate Graphics
    Mankato, Minnesota

Published & Distributed by:
    Plant Pics LLP
    P. O. Box 3224
    Duluth, MN 55803-3224

Book and cover design by:
    Clayton & Michele Oslund

Cover photos:
    Composite of pages 52, 86, 93 & 259

ISBN: 0-9667399-1-4

About the Authors

"Retirement is worth working for" has been their motto! Clayton and Michele are retired educators and perennial nursery people: Michele, a former music teacher and long-time gardener; Clayton a botany/horticulture professor. Plants and gardening are a passion with them. When the demands of the work world eased, their curiosity about plants combined with dreams of writing a book. A guide book about Hawaiian Gardens, *Hawaiian Gardens are to Go to* was their first. Photography and writing quickly got into their blood. Here is their second book!

Michele and Clayton Oslund

Acknowledgements

We treasure all the encouragement and patience from family and friends!

Our photographic excursions took us far and wide, but especially to many of the State and city parks, forests, hiking trails, bogs and roadsides of Northeastern Minnesota. People generously shared their knowledge and insight, directing us to plants and places we would not have found on our own. Special thanks to DNR and State Park staff members, naturalists and rangers who helped us and shared maps, plant phenology reports, check lists and other data about the flora of the area.

We are especially grateful for the encouragement and assistance of Retta James-Gasser, Naturalist, Gooseberry Falls State Park; Patricia Gordon, Naturalist, Banning State Park, and Linda Rademecky, Naturalist, along with interns Reghann LaFrance and Amber Peterson, St. Croix State Park; to Billy Larson for his expertise and time spent with us finding plants in bogs and marshlands; and to Deborah Pomroy-Petry for assistance at the Olga Lakala Herbarium, University of Minnesota, Duluth.

Clayton & Michele

To everyone who takes time to stop,

Enjoy the flowers!

Name, Rank and Plant Family

Plant names are often thought to be difficult. This is due in part to the thousands of plants we encounter in many aspects of life. We learn plant names to identify fruits and vegetables in our gardens and grocery stores. There are multitudes of trees, shrubs, flowering perennials, annuals and some plants we designate as weeds in our fields, pastures, lawns and gardens, and they all have names. When we come to parks, forests and other natural areas there are even more species!

Grouping plants helps the recognition process. At the grocery produce department, let's consider some lettuces: Head, bib, cos, romaine, and leaf lettuce are a few examples in the "lettuce group." Among other flowering plants in the garden, we may have planted several kinds of lilies including Asiatic, Day, Oriental, Tiger and Wood Lilies. Each group (Lettuce or Lily) is a collection of individual types that have characteristics in common.

Plants have common and scientific (botanical or Latin) names. Using the lily group as an example, "Wood Lily" is a common name and *Lilium philadelphicum* the scientific name for one individual type. Each individual plant type has a genus and species name; *Lilium* is the genus and *philadelphicum* the species name.

Family names are based primarily on flower and fruit structure. Other factors such as stem, leaf or root characteristics also give clues to grouping plants into families. A summary of plant families presented in this book is found on pages 296 to 300.

Scientific or botanical family names have an *aceae* (pronounced like the letters of the alphabet A-C-E) ending. *Liliaceae* is an example of the scientific family name for the group of plants we call lilies. Other names may not be so obvious, such as those of the Potato Family, also called Tomato, Nightshade or Tobacco Family. All of these belong to the *Solanaceae* Family. *Solanum tuberosum* is the genus and species name for "potato" in the *Solanaceae* Family. This sorting out of plants illustrates the need for scientific names. Often several common names are applied to one group of plants which can certainly become confusing.

Wood Lily
Lilium philadelphicum

Wildflower Watching

Tips on Using This Book

❋ Spring, Summer, Fall: Following the Pattern

Plants come and grow about the same time each season. For this reason, they are grouped by their bloom time, beginning with early spring flora. Changes in environment may cause plants to flower days earlier or be delayed. Once in bloom, some plants have flowers that last only a few days, while others display their flowers until frost-killed in late fall.

The *first five sections contain herbaceous plants*, arranged in a pattern from early spring continuing into autumn . Each of the next four sections, *Vines, Trees & Shrubs, Grasses & Sedges*, and *Ferns, Clubmosses and Horestails* are also organized by season. This pattern will not always be an accurate indication of the sequence of beginning bloom time because species vary a great deal on length of time they continue to bloom.

❋ Familiar Faces

It's easy to remember a face and forget the name! With the sequence pattern in mind, use this guide to find a photo of a plant you recognize. Next, page through other pictures in that time-frame. The plant in question may be at your fingertips.

❋ Companion Guides

No single book is *complete*: Every region has a unique plant population. Other books, based on keys and line drawings, may help to identify unknown plants. The authors suggest Newcomb's Wildflower Guide, listed in the bibliography, as a useful companion to this book. For more detail, the book by Gleason and Cronquist along with its illustrated companion by Holmgren are very useful.

✢ Discover Characteristics of Plant Families

Check out the information given about naming plants on page vii and in the Plant Family Facts section on pages 296-300.

➥ Noteworthy

Most pages have space for jotting down a note. For example, information on date, where seen, or other plants in the same location may help you remember where to find a favorite wild flower in the future.

Where to Find Them

Skunk Cabbage Fruits

Skunk Cabbage
Symplocarpus foetidus
Araceae (Arum) Family

Skunk Cabbage is one of the earliest spring flowers. As soon as water logged marshes (where it grows abundantly) thaw out in the spring, the plant sends up its mottled spathes (leaf-like coverings) which surround the spadix (floral spike). The flowers inside are visible for just a short while, and the spathes soon become hidden by large leaves as pictured below.

Nearly black fruits which resemble pineapples in shape (top left) develop and become exposed late in the season when autumn frosts kill the leaves.

The name "Skunk Cabbage" comes from the unmistakable odor of "skunk" when the leaves are crushed.

Jack-in-the-Pulpit, page 21. is another example of *spathe* and *spadix*.

Trailing Arbutus
Epigaea repens
Ericaceae (Heath) Family

Trailing Arbutus bloom season is early and short. Flowers are very fragrant. Its usual habitat is dry Pine forests.

Sadly Trailing Arbutus are becoming very hard to find because the plant is so sensitive to being disturbed such as when woodlands are logged or even when blossoms are picked.

Liverleaf is commonly referred to by its scientific name, *Hepatica*. There are two species which differ primarily by the shape of their leaves. *H. americana* has round lobes, and *H. acutiloba* has pointed lobes as pictured on page 3. Both species come in a range of colors, white, blue, violet and pink.

Liverleaf or Hepatica
Hepatica americana
Hepatica acutiloba
Ranunculaceae (Buttercup) Family

Hepatica americana Leaves

Hepatica are among the early spring ephemerals (plants that have flowers lasting only a few days or even just one day). Leaves may overwinter, turning a rusty brown color, or be packed down by snow, causing the flowers to poke up through fallen tree leaves. New green leaves soon appear after flowers have faded. Flowers appear to have 10 petals, but these are colored sepals (the first ring or whorl of parts on a flower). Many species of the Buttercup Family have flowers with colored sepals but no petals.

Hepatica acutiloba Leaves

Large-flowered Trillium
Trillium grandiflorum
Liliaceae (Lily) Family

Large-flowered Trillium is also called Large-white Trillium. By whatever name, the flowers turn shades of pink as they finish blooming and wither.

Large-flowered Trillium has three broad leaves that remain through summer and are held on a stem about 12 to 18 inches tall. Although flowers may vary in size, they all bloom above the leaves.

Another white *Trillium* in bloom at this time (not shown) is Snow or Dwarf White Trillium (*T. nivale*) which has narrow, more elliptical leaves.

Nodding Trillium flowers typically hang down under three broad leaves which are similar in shape to the leaves of *T. grandiflorum.* White flower petals curve backwards. Pink stamens are another identifying characteristic. Fleshy, bright-red berries usually develop after flowers fade. The yellow flower in the photo is Bluebead (page 17).

Purple Trillium (*T. erectum)* blooms later in the season (page 35).

Nodding Trillium
Trillium cernuum
Liliaceae (Lily) Family

Nodding Trillium Fruit

Gardening in the shade has become a popular practice, especially with many of these woodland wildflowers being introduced to the nursery trade by new propagating techniques or by being salvaged from wild areas designated to be destroyed by road building or commercial developments.

Several species of *Trillium* are now available from specialized nurseries and are useful in home landscapes as companions to *Hosta*, ferns, and other shade tolerant plants.

Bloodroot
Sanguinaria canadensis
Papaveraceae (Poppy) Family

Bloodroot capsules develop under
the canopy of leaves.

Bloodroot gets its name from reddish juice that exudes from the rhizomes (underground stems) when broken or cut. Flowers come very early and bloom before the leaves expand. Blossoms usually last only a few days but are worth the show. The crisp, white petals are harbingers of spring, to be sure. Shortly after the petals fall, a capsule (the fruit) forms containing several reddish-brown seeds. Each seed has a white, fleshy band (called an aril or eliasome) extending over one side. This aril is food for ants that disperse the seeds, propagating bloodroot plants naturally.

Bloodroot is another good plant for naturalizing in a home shade garden landscape. Plants are easy to propagate from seed if seeds are gathered fresh and planted before they dry out. If the aril dries, germination may be delayed for a year or the seed may die. Please use nursery propagated plants or find friends that have bloodroot and trade plants or seeds with them.

Bellwort
Uvularia grandiflora
Liliaceae (Lily) Family

Bellwort (above) grows to about 12 to 18 inches tall. It typically looks wilted when the leaves are expanding and while it is blooming. Once the bloom period is over, the leaves and stems become more erect and take on an appearance similar to Solomon's-seal.

Wild Oats (right) is shorter, only 6 to 12 inches in height. Flowers are smaller, creamy colored and have more blunt tips on the petals than *U. grandiflora*.

Wild Oats or Sessile Bellwort
Uvularia sessilifolia
Liliaceae (Lily) Family

Miterwort (left)
Mitella diphylla
Saxifragaceae (Saxifrage) Family

Miterwort is also called Bishop's Cap, a name derived from the shape of the flower. Tiny flowers with five delicate fringes have a dainty appearance. Uppermost leaves are opposite and sessile (not having stalks or petioles). Slightly lobed, heart-shaped basal leaves have petioles. The leaf in the lower right corner of the photo is not Miterwort but is Large-leaved Aster (page 208) which is commonly found in the same habitat.

Early Meadow Rue (right)
Thalictrum dioicum
Ranunculaceae (Buttercup) Family

Flowers of Early Meadow Rue dangle from the upper portion of the plant like miniature decorative ornaments shimmering in the breezes. Yellow anthers are the most conspicuous part of these tiny flowers.

Lyre-leaved Rock Cress (above)
Arabis lyrata
Brassicaceae (Mustard) Family

Lyre-leaved Rock Cress is a delicate, weak-stemmed plant about 5 to 10 inches tall. The basal leaves are deeply lobed (see inset), while the leaves on the upper stem are small and linear.

Smooth Rock Cress grows 1 to 3 feet in height. Basal leaves are somewhat lobed and upper linear leaves have small lobes that clasp the stem.

Smooth Rock Cress (left)
Arabis laevigata
Brassicaceae (Mustard) Family

9

Yellow Corydalis
Corydalis flavula
Papaveraceae (Poppy) Family

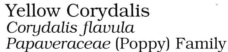

Yellow Corydalis is another woodland perennial that has found its way into gardeners' landscapes. With lovely lacy foliage, this plant stays attractive right through the summer. Yellow Corydalis purchased at a nursery will usually be a European species, *C. lutea*, which has larger flowers.

Another *Corydalis*, *C. aurea* or Golden Corydalis, is also found in this area. It takes a trained eye to distinguish a difference in the flowers. *C. flavula* has a small toothed crest on the upper petal and a shorter spur than *C. aurea*. Pale Corydalis with a pink flower (page 218) blooms later in the season.

Classification of the *Corydalis* genus is listed by some authors as being in the *Fumariaceae* or Fumitory Family, along with *Dicentra* (page 16).

Golden Alexanders
Zizia aurea
Apiaceae (Parsley) Family

Golden Alexanders resembles Wild Parsnip (page 126). A look at the leaves shows that they are doubly compound leaves with each of 3 leaflets divided again 3 to 7 times. Wild Parsnip has leaves divided into 5 to 15 leaflets that are not further subdivided.

Full sun in a meadow as well as shade at the forest's edge can be habitat for Golden Alexanders. It often shares it's woodland habitat with ferns.

Spring Beauty
Claytonia virginica
Portulacaceae (Purslane) Family

There are two very similar species of Spring Beauty. The major difference is in the leaves with *C. virginica* having narrow, linear leaves and *C. caroliniana* having broader leaves. Flowers of both, borne on short, weak stems, show colors that may be shaded from white to pink.

Moist woodlands are common habitat. After blooming, leaves die down and disappear by mid-summer.

Carolina Spring Beauty
Claytonia caroliniana
Portulacaceae (Purslane) Family

Wild Lily-of-the-Valley
Maianthemum canadense
Liliaceae (Lily) Family

Wild Lily-of-the-Valley typically has two leaves (occasionally three). The flower has four radiating points, an identifying characteristic.

Three-leaved False Solomon's-seal, a confusing look-alike (not illustrated), always has six points to its flower and normally has three leaves.

Fruits of Wild Lily-of-the-Valley (above) begin to develop shortly after flowering, first becoming white berries mottled with small red spots. In the fall, the berries turn to a pale red color.

Leaves of the early spring plants, with flower stalks just developing, create the mat-forming ground cover seen in the photo at left.

13

Wild Ginger
Asarum canadense
Aristolochiaceae (Birthwort) Family

Large, heart-shaped leaves help make Wild Ginger easy to identify in its woodland habitat. It prefers soils rich in nutrients.

Its unusual flowers are quite inconspicuous at the base of the plant and can be observed only by pushing the leaves aside.

Wild Ginger is often used in shade landscapes of home gardens. This and several other ginger species are commercially propagated and available at many garden centers and mail-order nurseries.

These gingers are not the source of the "spice" ginger which comes from a plant grown in tropical climates.

Wood Strawberry
Fragaria vesca
Rosaceae (Rose) Family

Similar at first glance, Wood Strawberry (above) has seeds on the surface of the berry while Common Strawberry (below) has seeds imbedded in pits within the red receptacle that makes up the strawberry fruit. The leaves of *F. vesca* are somewhat more pointed than in *F. virginiana*.

Common Strawberry
Fragaria virginiana
Rosaceae (Rose) Family

15

Marsh Marigold
Caltha palustris
Ranunculaceae (Buttercup) Family

Marsh Marigold is usually found growing in shallow water ditches, quiet lake shores and ponds or wet, marshy areas. It can tolerate soils that are not soggy wet, and, like many other native plants, are used in woodland landscaping. Nurseries can propagate this plant quite easily, making it available for the homeowner.

Dutchman's-breeches
Dicentra cucullaria
Papaveraceae (Poppy) Family

Delicate flowers are very short lived. To catch a glimpse of this delightful plant, it is necessary to keep a vigil in early spring. The flower shape is a clue on what led to its name "Dutchman's-breeches."

Some authors classify Dutchman's-breeches in the Bleeding-heart or Fumitory Family (*Fumariaceae*). *Corydalis* on page 10 is another member of this family.

Bluebead
Clintonia borealis
Liliaceae (Lily) Family

Bluebead is easy to recognize *in the fall.* Its brilliant blue fruit is an absolute give-away. In some areas it is known as Corn Lily.

When the broad leaves come up early in the spring, surrounding the flower stalk, the plant may be confused with Wild Leek (page 44). Distinctive yellow flowers bloom on a slender stalk and clearly identify this as Bluebead.

Blue is the predominant color in violets. There are over 80 species reported in North America, and differences in species are often very subtle, making them difficult to identify. Downy Blue Violet is identified by a white throat and "beards" on the two side petals which extend into the white throat. Purple stripes accent the lower petal.

Violets are drought tolerant but also thrive in moist soil habitats.

Dog Violet
Viola conspersa
Violaceae (Violet) Family

Several species of violets have prominent spurs protruding from the base of the lower petal. Dog Violet has a somewhat blunt spur. Its leaves are broad and heart-shaped. Long Spurred Violets boast a more slender spur.

Long Spurred Violet
Viola selkirkii
Violaceae (Violet) Family

Downy Blue Violet
Viola sororia
Violaceae (Violet) Family

There are fewer species of yellow and white violets within the scope of the Great Lakes region in comparison with the blues. Downy Yellow Violet has broad heart-shaped leaves that are fuzzy on the underside. The flower stalks arise along the stem and are short and fuzzy. It grows in dry woodlands. Canada Violet is a common white violet. A light-purplish tinge on the back of the upper two petals will identify *V. canadensis*. Its flower stalks originate on the stem.

Downy Yellow Violet
Viola pubescens
Violaceae (Violet) Family

Canada Violet
Viola canadensis
Violaceae (Violet) Family

Wild Sarsaparilla
Aralia nudicaulis
Araliaceae (Ginseng) Family

Sarsaparilla sends up a leaf stalk from a rhizome (underground stem). Shortly afterward, a stalk bearing 3 or 4 round clusters of greenish-white flowers appears. As the summer progresses, blue-black berries develop (right).

Its large, spicy-aromatic rhizome can be collected in the fall. An extract from this plant, along with others in the ginseng family, has been used as an ingredient in making root beer or a tea for medicinal purposes. The sarsaparilla extract of commerce for making root beer actually comes from a tropical species of Greenbrier *(Smilax)*, page 238.

The Arum Family has an unusual flower arrangement. Tiny, almost inconspicuous, flowers are borne on a pencil-like stalk called the spadix. The spadix is surrounded by a sheath called a spathe. In Jack-in-the-Pulpit, the spathe bends forward over the spadix nearly hiding the flowers on the spadix inside. There are variations in the color of the spathe from plant to plant. It may be green or have purplish stripes. Some authors separate the variants into three different species.

The fanciful spring spathe disappears when clusters of bright green berries form on the spadix in summer. By fall the berries turn bright red. Each berry has one or more seeds. Two small seedlings from a previous year's seeds are shown in the photo at the right.

Wild Calla (page 23) and Skunk Cabbage (page 1) are examples of plants in the Arum Family.

Jack-in-the-Pulpit
Arisaema triphyllum
Araceae (Arum) Family

Wood Anemone
Anemone quinquefolia
Ranunculaceae
(Buttercup) Family

Wood Anemone blankets the forest floor in localized areas. It is one of several flowers that is referred to as "Mayflower." Flowers are usually white, but may be tinged with pink. Being in the Buttercup Family, the showy *Anemone* flower parts are sepals as is the case with *Hepatica* on page 2.

False Rue Anemone is also lacking petals, having 5 showy white sepals. The leaves are similar to *Thalictrum* in appearance. (*Thalictrum*, pages 8 and 69).

False Rue Anemone
Isopyrum biternatum
Ranunculaceae
(Buttercup) Family

Wild Calla is usually found growing in shallow water in bogs or edges of ponds or lakes. The pure white spathe surrounds a golden colored spadix which produces a cluster of small green fruits (see yellow arrow) that turn red later in the season.

Wild Calla
Calla palustris
Araceae (Arum) Family

Wild Blue Phlox is often used in home landscaping to naturalize an area. It is available from specialty nurseries. Another name commonly given to this plant is Woodland Phlox.

Blue Phlox
Phlox divaricata
Polemoniaceae (Phlox) Family

Also called Creeping Charlie or Ground Ivy, Gill-over-the-Ground is a notorious weed. It has become a bane to homeowners whose lawns and gardens are in somewhat shaded areas. Another Eurasian species, it is naturalized throughout the Great Lakes Region and beyond. To its credit, the blue blossoms are quite pretty.

Gill-over-the-ground
Glechoma hederacea
Lamiaceae (Mint) Family

Each May Apple plant has only one white pendulant flower extending from the crotch of two large leaves. The flower produces one large berry 1 to 2 inches long. Fruit ripens to yellow and is edible fresh. Please take caution with the rest of the plant as the resins are toxic.

A favorite of shade gardeners, May Apples grow well in heavily shaded areas and naturalize easily. They are available from specialty nurseries.

May Apple or Mandrake
Podophyllum peltatum
Berberidaceae (Barberry) Family

The name Mandrake has been applied to May Apple, but the historical Mandrake is *Mandragora,* in the *Solanaceae* family, and was grown for medicinal purposes generations ago. *Mandragora* root was thought to mimic human form. According to the "Doctrine of Signatures," the root was useful in curing disease or treating a part of the human body that it resembled.

Mandragora species are native to the Mediterranean and Himalaya regions.

Trout Lilies are also called Dog Tooth Violets or Adder's Tongue.

White Trout Lily
Erythronium albidum
Liliaceae (Lily) Family

These early spring plants pop up in thick masses, each with one flower stalk sandwiched between two leaves. Once it has flowered and produced its seeds, the entire plant disappears by early summer. It grows well in shady home gardens that simulate a rich woods. Nurseries supply the small corms for propagating the plants. It may take two seasons to get a flowering-size plant. Once established, they multiply easily.

Yellow Trout Lily
Erythronium americanum
Liliaceae (Lily) Family

Similar to the Ginseng used as an herbal remedy (page 235), this dwarf form, only 4 to 8 inches tall, is found in nutrient-rich soils of moist wooded areas. The rounded umbel begins to develop as a tight cluster of buds (below). With lengthening of the flower stalk, the umbel expands into a delicate cluster of white flowers. Yellow berries develop later.

Dwarf Ginseng
Panax trifolius
Araliaceae (Ginseng) Family

Dwarf Ginseng has three compound leaves each of which may have 3 to 5 leaflets. The plants above have 3 large and 2 small leaflets.

Baneberrys grow from 1 to 2 feet tall and produce either red or white berries in the fall. Both types bloom with white flowers. White Baneberry has a slightly elongated flower cluster while Red Baneberrys have a more rounded cluster.

Both plants are reported to be poisonous. However, Naegele in *Edible and Medicinal Plants of the Great Lakes Region* reports that he has eaten the berries without feeling ill effects. He notes that the berries are so bitter, it is improbable that anyone would eat more than one.

Doll Eyes or White Baneberry
Actea pachypoda
Ranunculaceae (Buttercup) Family

The name "Doll Eyes" comes from the black spot on the end of the shiny, white berry.

Red Baneberry
Actea rubra
Ranunculaceae (Buttercup) Family

Baneberry is effective in woodsy landscapes. When several are planted close
together, they appear to clump as one
large, showy, "shrub-like" plant in the
summertime.

Nurseries which supply perennials often
offer Baneberry.

A zig-zag stem suggests the name Twisted Stalk. Its leaves resemble those of Solomon's-seal and False Solomon's-seal. Branching stems are a typical growth pattern. An abundance of mottled- rose, bell-shaped flowers arise from the base of the leaves. Bright red berries develop, but soon drop off or are eaten by critters of the forest.

Rose Twisted Stalk
Streptopus roseus
Liliaceae (Lily) Family

Swamp Saxifrage
Saxifraga pensylvanica
Saxifragaceae
  (Saxafrage) Family

A whorl of oval, blunt leaves at its base is a good clue to the identity of this plant. Flower stalks develop which sometimes grow to be over three feet tall. Flowers may vary from the cream color shown here to white or even a light shade of purple.

31

Field Pussytoes (opposite page)
Antennaria neglecta
Asteraceae (Aster) Family

Pussytoes are woolly plants that have mostly leafless scapes (flower stalks) and are usually less than 12 inches tall. There are several species which are difficult to distinguish without technical expertise.

Some authors call Pussytoes "Everlastings." Another plant *Anaphalis margaritacea* (Pearly Everlasting) has flowers similar to Pussytoes but grows taller (page 167).

Male and female flowers are produced on separate plants with most plants being female. Seeds will form even though the female flower is not pollinated (parthenogenesis).

Key to photos:
1 & 2 Female (pistillate) seed forming flowers
3 Male (staminate) flowers
4 Mature seeds which are wind borne
5 Mat of leaves after flowering

Early Sweet Coltsfoot (above)
Petasites palmatus
Asteraceae (Aster) Family

Growing in well-drained but wet soil, Early Sweet Coltsfoot produces a flower shoot up to 2 feet tall from an underground stem before leaves appear. The flower stalk has leaf-like bracts. Male and female flowers are found on separate plants.

After blooming, basal leaves appear which are 4 to 6 inches in diameter and have 5 to 7 deeply cut lobes.

A sturdy low-growing plant up to 12 inches tall, its stem and leaves are hairy (pubescent). Notice the deeply lobed, lance-shaped leaves. Dense clusters of yellow (or sometimes reddish) flowers bloom their way up the flower stalk over a period of 2 to 3 weeks. Its habitat is dry, open woods.

Wood Betony or Lousewort
Pedicularis canadensis
Scrophulariaceae (Snapdragon) Family

"Lousewort" is a name that translates as *louse plant*. It is applied to about 30 species of *Pedicularis*. According to folklore, it was believed that cattle and sheep would get lice when they came into contact with the plants.

Later blooming than other Trilliums common to the area (pages 4, 5 & 286), Purple Trillium grows up to 2 feet tall. Even though the species name, *T. erectum*, would seem to indicate that the flowers stand erect, they more often appear to droop as seen below. White to cream colored flowers are variations within the species.

Purple Trillium may be found in more southerly parts of the Great Lakes region.

Purple or Red Trillium
Trillium erectum
Liliaceae (Lily) Family

Spreading Dogbane
Apocynum androsaemifolium
Apocynaceae (Dogbane) Family

A shrubby-looking herbaceous perennial growing up to 4 feet tall, Spreading
Dogbane shows off spring-time finery
with bell-like, pink-striped blossoms.
Its stems are reddish-brown and contain a milky sap. This sap may cause
dermatitis.

36

Large Yellow Lady's-slipper
Cypripedium calceolus var. *pubescens*
Orchidaceae (Orchid) Family

Yellow Lady's-slipper is one of the more common orchids across the region. It is usually found in hardwood forests but also grows in swampy areas and meadow-like habitats. There are two variations of *Cypripedium calceolus;* variety *pubescens*, the Large Yellow Lady's-slipper, and variety *parviflorum* or Small Yellow Lady's-slipper. Variety *parviflorum* differs by having a smaller pouch and darker red petals and sepals.

Showy Lady's-slipper
Cypripedium reginae
Orchidaceae (Orchid) Family

Adapted to a wide range of habitats, the Showy Lady's Slippers can be found in coniferous and hardwood swamps and wet meadows. It is also found in roadside ditches that have been undisturbed for many years, growing in direct sunlight. Being a long-lived plant, it produces a larger clump each year.

This is Minnesota's State Flower.

A rare variation is the albino or white form.

White Showy
Lady's-slipper
Cypripedium reginae
var. albolabium

The fruit of the orchid, a dry capsule (below), is filled with dust-like seed. Typical of orchids, these seeds do not have an endosperm or food reserve. To germinate and grow, the embryonic plant needs to have a partnership with a fungus in the soil that provides food while the young plant is developing. Several years of underground development takes place before the orchid sends shoots above ground. Wild orchids usually do not survive transplanting.

Pink Lady's-slipper or Moccasin-flower
Cypripedium acaule
Orchidaceae (Orchid) Family

One of the most common of the temperate climate slipper orchids, look for it in shaded habitats from dry sandy forests to wet bogs and swamps.

Sometimes called Stemless Lady's-slipper, this plant has a long flower stalk which comes up between two basal leaves growing from the crown of the plant.

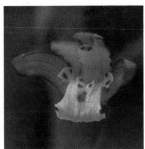

Spotted Coral Root
Corallorhiza maculata
Orchidaceae (Orchid) Family

What, no green leaves? Most orchids have green leaves to conduct photosynthesis, but *Corallorhiza* species rely on a symbiotic relationship with a fungus for all their nourishment, not just during embryonic development, but during the entire life of the plant! The fungus gets its nourishment from digesting decaying organic material in the soil. In an intimate relationship with the orchid's roots or rhizome, the fungus transfers the nourishment to the orchid.

Spotted Coral Root is widely distributed through out northeastern U. S. and southeastern Canada. Other *Corallorhiza* that may be found in this region include Striped Coral Root *(C. striata)* and Early Coral Root *(C. trifida)*.

Buckbean
Menyanthes trifoliata
Gentianaceae
  (Gentian) Family

Common to Sphagnum peat bogs, muddy lake shores and shallow water ponds, Buckbean exhibits its lovely cluster of white blossoms held above three large, oval-shaped leaves.

Yellow Water Buttercup
Ranunculus flabellaris
Ranunculaceae (Buttercup) Family

Characteristic to this aquatic species, most of the plant's finely divided leaves are submerged. Leaves that are above water are less divided. Small yellow flowers are held above the water's surface. Quiet water of ponds or bays is the usual habitat.

Another name given to this species is Yellow Water-crowfoot.

Now found in marshes and wet roadsides, Yellow Iris has escaped from home gardens. It is a European native that has become naturalized.

Yellow Iris (below)
Iris pseudacorus
Iridaceae (Iris) Family

White Mandarin or Twisted Stalk
Streptopus amplexifolius
Liliaceae (Lily) Family

Larger than Rose Twisted Stalk (page 30), White Mandarin has a similar structure. A major identifying characteristic is the twisted peduncle (flower stalk) shown left. Flowers are creamy-white to green. Red fruits develop in mid- to late summer. Fine hairs on the lower stem, shown in the upper left photo, are another clue to its identity.

Wild Leek
Allium tricoccum
Liliaceae (Lily) Family

Wild Leek first appears in the spring with two broad basal leaves. As the flowers begin to open, the leaves wither. Only shriveled remnants are left behind.

Leeks, in the *Allium* genus along with onions and garlic, are listed as being in *Amaryllidaceae* or the Amaryllis Family according to some references.

Flower Stalk with Bud

Early Spring Leaves

White Pea or Pale Vetchling
Lathyrus ochroleucus
Fabaceae (Pea or Legume) Family

Creamy-white flowers and compound leaves, usually with 6 egg-shaped leaflets, identify White Pea. Tendrils are found at the tip of the leaves.

Small-flowered Crowfoot
Ranunculus abortivus
Rununculaceae (Buttercup) Family

Tiny yellow petals and sepals surround a green button-like cluster of reproductive parts at the center of the flower.

The "crowfoot" leaves are on the upper part of the stem. Roundish, toothed leaves are found at the base of the plant. Small-flowered Crowfoot may grow up to 24 inches tall but is often as short as 6 inches.

Star Flower
Trientalis borealis
Primulaceae (Primula) Family

At the top of a short, sturdy stem, Star Flower has a whorl of 5 to 10 leaves and two star-like white flowers blooming at the center.

Count the petals. (Normally there are seven!) Few species have flower parts in multiples of seven, making them a rarity.

Golden Ragwort
Senecio aureus
Asteraceae (Aster) Family

Golden Ragwort is characterized by a flat-topped flower cluster, finely cut upper leaves, and rounded leaves at its base. Growing 1 to 3 feet tall, its common habitat is wet meadows and swampy areas.

Purple or Water Avens
Geum rivale
Rosaceae (Rose) Family

Nodding flowers with purplish sepals and yellow petals hang atop long stems that have small leaves divided into 3 segments. Basal leaves have 3 large segments at the tip with several smaller leaflets along the rachis (midrib). Purple Avens is found in wet habitats.

Virginia Bluebell
Mertensia virginica
Boraginaceae (Borage) Family

Blooming takes place over a prolonged period from spring to early summer. Flower color changes from pink when in bud to blue when fully open. Once flowering is over, the leaves wither and disappear. Egg-shaped leaves are alternately arranged on a stem growing 1 to 2 feet tall. Virginia Bluebells make a lovely show in a shady home landscape.

Winter Cress
Barbarea spp.
Brassicaceae (Mustard) Family

These Cresses are examples of Mustard Family plants that "pop up" in many places as weeds, especially common in agricultural crops. Carried by birds and other means, mustard seeds are spread throughout the region.

Yellow Cress
Rorippa spp.
Brassicaceae (Mustard) Family

Sheep, Field or Common Sorrel
Rumex acetosella
Polygonaceae (Buckwheat) Family

Sheep Sorrel is a wide-spread plant of European origin. It has become naturalized throughout the region and is a persistent weed in many fields and gardens. It spreads by rhizomes and by seeds and grows in wet as well as dry soils, in nutrient rich soil as well as poor.

Attractive, spear-shaped leaves have flaring lobes at their base. Sheep Sorrel, with its reddish inflorescence, makes a dramatic appearance as ground cover.

Common Groundsel
Senecio vulgaris
Asteraceae (Aster) Family

Common Groundsel has golden-yellow flowers in heads that do not fully open. Bracts surrounding the flower heads have black tips. Flowers continue to bloom throughout the summer, producing multiple generations of seeds in one season. Leaves are long and deeply lobed. Native to Europe, it has naturalized throughout the Great Lakes region and has become a tenacious weed.

Wild Columbine
Aquilegia canadensis
Ranunculaceae
          (Buttercup) Family

Columbines are distinctive with long spurs extending backward on their petals. The sepals in Wild Columbine are red and showy, extending forward between each of the petals which are yellow and blunt in front.

Habitats of Wild Columbine range from woods to open meadows and as landscape plants in home gardens.

"Domestic" columbines constitute a wide collection of other species and hybrids. Plants with large blooms in many color choices are now available commercially.

Bird's-eye Primrose is a general name for primroses that have the yellow "eye". *P. mistassinica* is also called Dwarf Canadian Primrose. It is characteristically only a few inches high and commonly grows in cracks among rocks as seen above. These were found on a rocky, north shore cliff of Lake Superior.

Bird's-eye Primrose (above)
Primula mistassinica
Primulaceae (Primrose) Family

Butterwort (left)
Pinguicula vulgaris
Lentibulariaceae (Bladderwort) Family

Thriving in the same habitat as Bird's-eye Primrose, these tiny Butterwort plants trap insects! Its curled leaf is the natural appearance. A slimy covering, feeling "greasy" to touch, attracts and traps small insects. The leaves then roll up and digest the insects. Bon appetit!

Seed capsules (below) illustrates the "Cranes-bill" shape which gives the plant its name. The seeds are in the "knob" (or carpel) at the end of the curls. Each flower has 3 to 5 of these curls that pop free from the capsule to disperse the seed.

Wild Geranium
or Spotted Cranesbill
Geranium maculatum
Geraniaceae (Geranium) Family

Wild Geranium, a common woodland plant, grows up to 2 feet high. Along with several other *Geranium* species and hybrid cultivars, it has been domesticated for home gardens.

Aniseroot and Sweet Cicely are look-alike plants. They have dry fruits or "seeds" similar to but longer than a dill seed found in your kitchen spice rack. These fruits stick to clothing and the fur of animals, a method the plant uses to disperse the seed.

Umbels of tiny white flowers, smooth stems and deeply lobed leaves are typical of Aniseroot. Sweet Cicely *(O. claytoni)*, not pictured, has shorter styles in its flowers, shorter fruits and hairy leaves and stems.

Aniseroot
Osmorhiza longistylis
Apiaceae (Parsley) Family

Strikingly beautiful, often seen in a meadow or open woods, the Indian Paintbrush shows off its brightly colored bracts. Orange-red is the most common color, but occasionally a plant with yellow bracts may be found. Greenish-yellow flowers are inconspicuous, remaining nearly hidden by the bracts. It grows 1 to 2 feet tall and has forked leaves along a single stem.

Indian Paintbrush or Painted Cup
Castilleja coccinea
Scrophulariaceae (Snapdragon) Family

Hoary Puccoon
Lithospermum canescens
Boraginaceae (Forget-me-not) Family

This herbaceous perennial is found in dry, open or wooded areas. Its rich, golden color is especially eye-catching on roadsides. Stems grow 12 to 18 inches tall, and like the rest of the plant, are covered with fine hairs.

A name given by the Indians, "puccoon" relates to red dye which can be extracted from the roots.

Honewort (above)
Cryptotaenia canadensis
Apiaceae (Parsley) Family

A typical characteristic of Honewort is the unequal length of the rays of the umbel. Each small cluster of flowers has a stalk of varying length. It has a compound leaf with each leaflet showing a different lobe pattern.

Shepherd's Purse
Capsella bursa-pastoris
Brassicaceae (Mustard) Family

Shepherd's Purse is another European introduction now naturalized in North America. In addition to being found in open woods and native meadows, it is a persistent weed in fields and gardens. The name comes from the shape of the dry, triangular fruits resembling a pouch or bag used by a shepherd.

False Solomon's-seal
Smilacina racemosa
Liliaceae (Lily) Family

False Solomon's-seal can be recognized by the cluster of white flowers at the tip of the stem. Fruits from these flowers become bright red in autumn.

Leaves and stem are look-alikes to true Solomon's-seal (page 138). Habitat of each of these species is similar. Light shade of woodlands with nutrient rich soil is ideal for them to flourish.

Like Solomon's-seal, False Solomon's-seal is used in home landscaping in woodland settings. It is widely available in perennial nurseries.

Another species of *Smilacina*, Starry False Solomon's-seal, is described on page 74.

Grove Sandwort is a low-growing perennial that thrives in open wooded areas. Fragile-looking stems may support one or more flowers.

These plants spread by underground rhizomes, forming a patch.

The photo below shows Grove Sandwort growing along with Wild Lily-of-the-Valley.

Grove Sandwort
Arenaria lateriflora
Caryophyllaceae
(Pink) Family

Growing to 3 feet tall, this Buttercup has showy golden-yellow flowers with overlapping petals. The stem is usually hairy. Lower leaves are deeply cut into several lobes and are larger than those higher on the stem.

Open forests and meadows are common habitat.

Tall or Common Buttercup
Ranunculus acris
Ranunculaceae (Buttercup) Family

Swamp Buttercup
Ranunculus septentrionalis
Ranunculaceae (Buttercup) Family

Swamp Buttercup differs from Tall Buttercup by having compound leaves with short stalks on the leaflets. The rounded leaves under the compound leaves in the photo above are Marsh Marigold leaves.

As the name indicates, Swamp Buttercup thrives in wet woods and meadows, growing to about 3 feet tall.

Canada Anemone
Anemone canadensis
Ranunculaceae (Buttercup) Family

One of the most common Anemones, it spreads by long underground stems, often producing large patches once it gets established. Compare Wood Anemone (page 22) which is shorter and earlier blooming.

Canada Anemone favors damp woods and meadows and grows to about 18 inches tall. Compound leaves are stalkless.

Lesser Stitchwort
Stellaria graminea
Caryophyllaceae (Pink) Family

Dainty white flowers appear to hang in mid-air on thin stems, a typical growth pattern of Lesser Stitchwort. Belonging to the Pink Family, it has 5 petals that are cleft or partially divided, some cleft so deeply that it may look like 10 petals rather than 5 (photo lower right). Bright rusty red anthers stand out against the snow white petals. It is an alien species that has become naturalized and is quite common in grassy places.

Caraway
Carum carvi
Apiaceae (Parsley) Family

Fine-textured leaves and dainty white flowers in a small umbel characterize Caraway.

Aromatic seeds are used as seasoning in many foods, especially rye bread and cabbage dishes.

A native of Eurasia, Caraway has escaped from cultivation and now is found growing in road ditches and other dry, open places.

One of several species, this Hawksbeard has smooth, nearly leafless stems, thriving in sunny locations along roadsides. Annual Hawksbeard blooms later in the season (page 90).

Hawksbeard
Crepis spp.
Asteraceae (Aster) Family

Orange Hawkweed
Hieracium aurantiacum
Asteraceae (Aster) Family

Also a European native, Orange Hawkweed has spread throughout our region. It establishes itself quickly by stolons and forms dense mats. The leaves and stems are fuzzy. Unopened buds (left) have a deep purplish-black appearance.

Lupine
Lupinus spp.
Fabaceae (Pea or Legume) Family

Lupines (escaped from gardens) flourish in dry meadows and roadsides. Blue, pink and white are common colors. Wild Lupine, *Lupinus perennis* (not shown), has a smaller floral raceme and is generally blue.

Purple Meadow Rue grows to 5 feet tall on distinctively purple stems. Sometimes it is called Tall Meadow Rue.

Another species, *T. polygamum* (not pictured), has white, club-shaped flowers that do not droop. This species is also called Tall Meadow Rue.

Dangling flowers on the Purple Meadow Rue have white sepals, no petals and greenish-yellow stamens.

Purple or Tall Meadow Rue
Thalictrum dasycarpum
Ranunculaceae (Buttercup) Family

Beach Pea
Lathyrus japonicus
Fabaceae (Pea or Legume) Family

Found on sandy shores of the Great Lakes, eye-catching bicolored flowers stand out against its lush green foliage. Compound leaves have broad leaflets and large arrow-shaped stipules.

At first count, Black Snakeroot often appears to have 7 leaflets on the larger compound leaves. A closer look reveals that the side leaflets are cleft so deeply they each appear as two rather than one.

Flowers are greenish-white and form bristly burs with hooks.

Black Snakeroot
Sanicula marilandica
Apiaceae (Parsley) Family

71

Prairie Plantain
Plantago patagonica
Plantaginaceae (Plantain) Family

Prairie Plantain is found in open, dry, sandy shores of the Great Lakes regions. It grows to about 6 inches in height. Flowers are borne in silky, pubescent spikes. Leaves are covered with fine hairs. Prairie Plantain looks "woolly."

False Heather
Hudsonia tomentosa
Cistaceae (Rockrose) Family

False Heather mimics the scale-like leaves of true Heathers. With its natural ground-cover tendency, it grows into thick, shrubby mats about 8 inches deep. Bright yellow flowers form at the tips of the twigs.

Its habitat is the dry, sandy beaches and dunes of the Great Lakes.

Red berries form
in autumn.

Starry False Solomon's-seal
Smilacina stellata
Liliaceae (Lily) Family

Starry False Solomon's-seal is a miniature of its taller relative, *Smilacina racemosa* (page 59). Tolerating a wide range
of habitats, Starry False Solomon's-seal thrives on sunny
sand dunes of the Great Lakes to shaded, nutrient rich
woodlands. These durable little plants become a striking
ground cover in nature. Now commercially propagated, they
have found their way into home landscapes.

Mouse-eared Chickweed
Cerastium vulgatum
Caryophyllaceae (Pink) Family

Mouse-eared Chickweed has hairy stems. Flower petals have a typical cleft, trademark of the Pink Family. It can be a pesty weed in lawns and gardens as it spreads quickly once established.

Black Medic
Medicago lupulina
Fabaceae (Legume) Family

Black Medic has a sprawling growth habit. Yellow flowers form a tight cluster followed by black, coiled seed pods. Once established on roadsides, waste places, lawns and gardens it becomes an invasive weed.

Rough Cinquefoil
Potentilla norvegica
Rosaceae (Rose) Family

Identifying characteristics include a hairy stem, compound leaves with 3 leaflets (most cinquefoils have 5 - 7 leaflets), and green sepals extending out longer than the bright yellow petals. These tenacious plants may blossom when only a few inches tall or grow to 3 feet in height.

Norwegian Cinquefoil is another name for this plant.

Wood Sorrel
Oxalis stricta
Oxalidaceae (Wood-sorrel) Family

Wood Sorrel leaves are compound with 3 heart-shaped leaflets resembling clover leaves, and sometimes called Sour Clover due to the taste of high oxalic acid content in the leaves.

It is widespread on roadsides, open places, and areas of disturbed soil. There are several other species of Wood Sorrels including *O. violacea* (not pictured) with pink-purple flowers.

Yellow-eyed, bright blue flowers bloom on masses of deep green foliage, thriving on wet soils and even in shallow water.

Of European origin, it has escaped from gardens to become established in many different regions.

Forget-me-not
Myosotis scorpioides
Boraginaceae (Forget-me-not) Family

Long-leaved Bluet
Houstonia longifolia
Rubiaceae (Bedstraw) Family

Bluet plants usually form clumps in dry, open wooded or rocky areas.

Clusters of white to light lavender flowers bloom on the stem tips.

Purple or American Vetch
Vicia americana
Fabaceae (Pea or Legume) Family

Purple Vetch typically has an open or loose cluster of flowers on a smooth stem that climbs by tendrils at the leaf tips. Leaflets are narrow and oblong. Look for a toothed stipule at the base of the leaves.

Bugle (left)
Ajuga reptans
Lamiaceae (Mint) Family

Bugle is a mat-forming plant about 8 inches high that spreads by leafy stolons. Now widely used in shade gardens as a ground cover, Bugle shows off its handsome leaves and lovely spring flowers. Brought over from Europe, it is another garden escapee, naturalizing throughout the region.

Ajuga is sometimes called Bugleweed, but another mint family plant, *Lycopus uniflorus* (page 229) is recognized as Bugleweed.

Twinleaf
Jeffersonia diphylla
Berberidaceae (Barberry) Family

The range of Twinleaf extends into more southerly regions covered by this book.

With its attractive foliage and eye-catching white flower, this woodland plant becomes a welcome addition to shade garden landscapes. It is now propagated and available in specialty nurseries.

As green fruits develop (below), leaves continue to elongate, covering up the fruit completely by late summer.

Dame's Rocket
Hesperis matronalis
Brassicaceae (Mustard) Family

Similar to garden Phlox in color and form, Dame's Rocket deserves to be recognized on its own merits. Being in the Mustard Family, the flowers have 4 petals. It also has a pleasant fragrance. Phlox has 5 petals and little fragrance.

Three-toothed Cinquefoil
Potentilla tridentata
Rosaceae (Rose) Family

Both of these Cinquefoils thrive on the rocky cliffs of Lake Superior's North Shore. Three-toothed Cinquefoil is recognized by compound leaves with 3 leaflets, each having 3 small "teeth" at the tip. Silvery Cinquefoil has 5 leaflets with white, woolly undersides. Leaflets are narrow with deep cut lobes looking like small oak leaves. Stems are fuzzy, too.

Silvery Cinquefoil
Potentilla argentea
Rosaceae (Rose) Family

Hooker's Orchid may be listed in the Genus *Habenaria* by other authors. Smith, in *Orchids of Minneosta*, reports that the current trend is to place terrestrial orchids, previously included in *Habenaria*, into the *Platanthera* genus. Other Orchids in this genus include *P. ciliaris* (page 143), *P. hyperborea* (page 122) and *P. psycodes* on page 168.

Hooker's Orchid
Platanthera hookeri
Orchidaceae (Orchid) Family

Upland pine forests are a common habitat for Hooker's Orchid, but it has been found in deciduous forests as well. The yellowish-green flowers bloom on a stalk about 8 to 15 inches tall.

Twinflower
Linnaea borealis
Caprifoliaceae
(Honeysuckle) Family

In the same pine forests that are home to Hooker's Orchid, Twinflower flourishes. These dainty bell-shaped blossoms come in pairs on a single slender stalk. The plants have a trailing habit, spreading into colonies.

Bird-on-the-wing or Gaywing
Polygala paucifolia
Polygalaceae (Milkwort) Family

Another denizen of pine forests, Bird-on-the-wing is named for the fanciful flowers which have the appearance of two birds flying in opposite directions. The quaint flowers may look orchid-like, but the plant is not an orchid.

Pink Pyrola
Pyrola asarifolia
Pyrolaceae (Wintergreen) Family

Pictured here are two examples of *Pyrola* species. Others have white flowers, one of which is later blooming and pictured on page 160. Pyrolas are found growing in pine forests among mosses and through pine needle mulch on the forest floor.

Greenish-flowered Pyrola (left)
Pyrola virens
Pyrolaceae (Wintergreen) Family

Blue Flag
Iris versicolor
Iridaceae (Iris) Family

Widely distributed throughout the region, Blue Flag fills the marshes and roadside ditches with dashes of color.

Poison Ivy
Rhus radicans
Anacardiaceae (Sumac or Cashew) Family

CAUTION

DO NOT
TOUCH!

Poison Ivy is known for three shiny leaflets. It is less well known for its clusters of white flowers which form light green berries as shown top right. The lower picture shows berries in the spring that have overwintered. Caution: leaves, stems, flowers and berries all contain skin irritant throughout the year.

89

Annual Hawksbeard is a weedy plant that has become naturalized from Europe. 12 to 18 inch stems support clusters of Dandelion-like flowers. Finely divided leaves are a trademark for identification of this plant. It grows in dry, sandy places. Another *Crepis* species is found on page 66.

Annual Hawksbeard
Crepis tectorum
Asteraceae (Aster) Family

Clusters of pink flowers give way to large milkweed seedpods. Packed inside the pod are seeds topped with tufts of silky hairs. Once the pod splits open, the tufted seeds become scattered with the wind.

Milkweed leaves are the favorite food of Monarch butterfly larvae. This black and yellow caterpillar eats its way across the leaves, while the plant seems oblivious to its role in the life cycle of the butterfly.

Common Milkweed
Asclepias syriaca
Asclepiadaceae (Milkweed) Family

Only subtle differences separate *Silene cserei* from *S. cucubalus* (facing page). Casual observation does not reveal that *S. cserei* is a biennial and *S. cucubalus* is perennial. Differences seen in the photos are due more to environment and stage of flower development than heredity.

These plants grow on dry, sandy or gravely areas such as roadsides and waste places.

Lesser Bladder Campion
Silene cserei
Caryophyllaceae (Pink) Family

Bladder Campion
Silene cucubalus
Caryophyllaceae (Pink) Family

White Campion
Silene latifolia
Caryophyllaceae (Pink) Family

White Campion is also called Evening Lychnis
and White Cockle. It has both male and female
flowers. Female flowers produce large inflated
capsules. White Campion is widely established
in fields, meadows and roadsides across North
America.

Similar to Beach Pea in color and form of plant (page 70), Purple Pea has flower clusters that are elongated and crowded with more blossoms.

Purple Pea is better adapted to a wider range of habitats, especially to wooded areas with light shade.

Purple Pea
Lathyrus venosus
Fabaceae
        (Pea or Legume) Family

Northern Bedstraw
Galium boreale
Rubiaceae (Bedstraw) Family

Northern Bedstraw has smooth, erect stems up to 2 feet tall. Narrow linear leaves are in whorls of 4 compared to other Bedstraws that have 6 leaves in a whorl (Rough Bedstraw, page 174). Flowers in tight clusters are abundant.

Wood Lily
Lilium philadelphicum
Liliaceae (Lily) Family

Vibrant orange petals stretch upward. Lance-shaped leaves are in whorls on the upper part of the stem but opposite on the lower stem. Meadows and open woods are ideal habitats.

Meadows, prairies and open woods are ideal habitats for Bastard Toadflax. Being in the Sandalwood Family, it follows the trait of attaching its roots to the roots of another plant in order to draw nutrients from its host. Even though it uses this parasitic attribute, Bastard Toadflax has chlorophyll, producing some of its own food as evidenced by its green leaves.

Bastard Toadflax (right)
Comandra umbellata
Santalaceae (Sandalwood) Family

Bird's-foot Trefoil is a handsome plant with showy yellow flowers that give way to slender seed pods. These pods look like a bird's foot, hence its name. It is a native of Europe that has naturalized in North America. Compound leaves have 5 leaflets, the lower two similar to stipules.

Bird's-foot Trefoil
Lotus corniculatus
Fabaceae (Pea or Legume) Family

One-flowered Wintergreen
Monesis uniflora
Pyrolaceae (Wintergreen) Family

Also called Wood Nymph, this miniature plant is only 2 to 5 inches tall. It has a rosette of evergreen leaves at the base of the flower stalk. Each plant supports one flower. Common habitat is coniferous woodlands.

Dragon's-mouth typically grows in Sphagnum bogs. It appears to be leafless while flowering. Only after the flower has withered does a single grass-like leaf appear. The species name *bulbosa* refers to its bulb-like corm.

Dragon's-mouth (below)
Arethusa bulbosa
Orchidaceae (Orchid) Family

Pitcher-plant
Sarracenia purpurea
Sarraceniaceae (Pitcher-plant) Family

Sphagnum peat bogs are common habitat for insect-eating Pitcher-plants (opposite page and above). A rosette of pitcher-shaped leaves at the base are partly filled with water. Insects make their way inside where they are trapped, digested and absorbed, providing nourishment to the plant.

Cow Parsnip
Heracleum maximum
Apiaceae (Parsley) Family

This giant herb may grow up to 8 feet and sometimes taller. Umbels of elegant white flowers in flat
clusters bloom at the top of the plant. Compound
leaves have 3 deeply-toothed leaflets. Its hollow stem
is up to 2 inches in diameter.

Water Hemlock
Cicuta maculata
Apiaceae
(Parsley) Family

Water Hemlock, a plant of wet ditches, swamps and meadows, grows from 3 to 6 feet tall. It is recognizable by its compound leaves with narrow lance-shaped, toothed leaflets. Some of the leaflets are twice or thrice compound. A hollow branching stem has streaks of purple.

CAUTION: The fleshy taproot is highly poisonous. It has been fatal to persons who have eaten it. Water Hemlock is similar to Water Parsnip, *Sium sauve*, a non-toxic plant (not pictured).

Bicknell's Cranesbill
Geranium bicknellii
Geraniaceae (Geranium) Family

Deeply-cut, lobed leaves and sprawling manner give a delicate air to this Geranium. It has loose clusters of small pink to light lavender flowers. This is a native plant that becomes a weed in many gardens.

Pineapple Weed
Matricaria matricarioides
Asteraceae (Aster) Family

Although native to Western North America, it has spread throughout the eastern regions becoming a prolific weed, especially unwanted in gardens.

Stems and leaves are aromatic, smelling like pineapple when crushed.

Flower heads are unusual by having only central disk flowers without showy ray flowers like daisies or asters.

Large-flowered Beardtounge likes sandy prairies, but it will take up residence in prairie-like habitats in the westerly and southerly Great Lakes regions. Beautiful flowers present themselves at the top of the stem. This perennial grows from 2 to 3 feet tall.

"Beardtounge" describes one of 5 stamens which is sterile (not producing pollen). In some species, this special stamen is covered with hairs (bearded).

Large-flowered Beardtounge
Penstemon grandiflorus
Scrophulariaceae (Snapdragon) Family

Cow or Tufted Vetch
Vicia cracca
Fabaceae (Pea or Legume) Family

Tufted Vetch, of Eurasian origin, is naturalized throughout this region, especially along roadsides and meadows. The plant is weak-stemmed and sprawling. Compound leaves are long with up to 10 narrow leaflets terminating in a tendril. Its inflorescence is long and one-sided having as many as 30 flowers.

Alfalfa, an Asian native, is another culti-vated plant for pasture and hay produc-tion throughout this region. It grows in clumps up to 3 feet tall. Purple to blue-violet flowers change into a spiral pod which has up to 3 full turns. Like other field crops, Alfalfa is also widely naturalized.

Alfalfa or Lucerne
Medicago sativa
Fabaceae (Pea or Legume) Family

Red Clover
Trifolium pratense
Fabaceae (Pea or Legume) Family

Red Clover, native to Europe, is widely cultivated as a pasture or hay crop and has also escaped cultivation to become naturalized. The magenta flowers are in compact round heads. Oval leaves usually show a pattern of white in the shape of a V.

Alsike Clover
Trifolium hybridum
Fabaceae (Pea or Legume) Family

White Clover
Trifolium repens
Fabaceae (Pea or Legume) Family

Alsike and White Clovers, like Red Clover, are cultivated plants of Eurasian origin, now widely distributed and naturalized.

These two clovers have similar flower heads. To tell them apart:

(1) White Clover has a pale, greenish-white crescent on its leaflets. Alsike leaflets are solid green.

(2) White Clover flower stalks and leaves grow up from creeping runners. Flowers and leaves of Alsike come from branching stems.

Heal-all
or Selfheal
Prunella vulgaris
Lamiaceae
   (Mint) Family

This native plant easily invades lawns, fields and roadsides with its spreading growth habit. Violet flowers are produced in dense heads. As its name suggests, it is still used as an herbal medicine.

Ox-eye Daisy
Chrysanthemum leucanthemum
Asteraceae (Aster) Family

Ox-eye Daisy establishes itself in meadows, roadsides and lawns, spreading by rootstocks and self-seeding. It is often seen in large patches or throughout an entire field. Left on its own, it may grow up to 3 feet tall.

"Fresh as a Daisy" Ox-eyes and Heal-all bloom through the transition of late spring into summer.

Valerian or Garden Heliotrope
Valeriana officinalis
Valerianaceae (Valerian) Family

Growing 2 to 3 feet tall, Valerian is topped with a compact cluster of white to pinkish flowers. In late summer, spent flowers drop off leaving behind a lacy-looking red residue (photo below). Leaves are deeply divided into lance-shaped segments.

Yellow Sweet Clover
Melilotus officinalis
Fabaceae (Pea or Legume) Family

Sweet clovers, yellow and white, are coarse-stemmed clovers used for hay and pasture. Because of their deep roots and nitrogen fixing process, both of these species produce a large amount of biomass, growing 2 to 4 feet tall. They are used for soil building by plowing them down as "green fertilizer" crop.

White Sweet Clover
Melilotus alba
Fabaceae (Pea or Legume) Family

Greater Bladderwort
Utricularia vulgaris
Lentibulariaceae (Bladderwort) Family

Underwater leaves have tiny "bladders" that trap and digest minute aquatic organisms as their food source. Flower stalks emerge above the water producing clusters of two-lipped yellow flowers. Quiet ponds or ditches with a continuous water supply are home to this water plant.

Narrow-leaved Cattail
Typha angustifolia
Typhaceae (Cattail) Family

Common Cattail
Typha latifolia
Typhaceae (Cattail) Family

Cattails are well-known plants of marshes and wet ditches. Two similar species can be identified quickly by a difference in their flower spikes. Male and female flowers of Narrow-leaved Cattail are separated by a gap (see arrow). Each Cattail has male flowers on the upper portion of the spike and female flowers on the lower part. Later in the season, after the female flowers have been pollinated, male flowers drop off leaving only the female spike to develop.

Turk's Cap Lily
Lilium superbum
Liliaceae (Lily) Family

Michigan Lily
Lilium michiganense
Liliaceae (Lily) Family

Turk's Cap Lilies inhabit the eastern part of the region covered by this book. Michigan Lilies are native to the westerly areas. Both species are quite similar.

Michigan Lilies are frequently called Turk's Cap, but they are not the same. Turk's Cap is the "star" of the show, displaying a green star in the markings of its throat. Turk's Cap also reaches superb heights, often as tall as 8 feet.

The trio of Michigan Lilies above exhibit spotted orange throat color without a green star. These equally splendid lilies may reach 5 feet in height.

Also called Western Salsify, this plant looks like a giant Dandelion especially when the large, yellow flowers turn into fluffy, globe-shaped seed heads with a 3 to 4 inch diameter. Like Dandelion seed, the wind scatters Yellow Goat's Beard to new locations.

Yellow Goat's Beard
Tragopogon dubius
Asteraceae (Aster) Family

Blue-eyed Grass (below)
Sisyrinchium montanum
Iridaceae (Iris) Family

Names can be misleading. This grassy-leaved plant has *yellow eyes!* Small blue flowers are made up of sepals and petals that look alike (tepals). Each tepal has a distinctive bristle-like tip.

It thrives in grassy meadows, making it hard to find when not in blossom.

Daisy or Common Fleabane
Erigeron philadelphicus
Asteraceae (Aster) Family

Erigeron species, called Fleabanes, are aster-like plants usually blooming earlier than Asters. Ray flowers are more numerous in Fleabanes. *E. philadelphicus* may have over 100 pink rays. Central disk flowers are yellow. Compare Lesser Daisy Fleabane, *E. strigosus*, on page 150.

117

Rabbit's Foot Clover
Trifolium arvense
Fabaceae (Pea or Legume) Family

Rabbit's Foot Clover lines miles of roadsides in some regions. Its soft, silky, pinkish-gray heads appear on low 4 to 12 inch plants. A European immigrant, it is an annual, reseeding itself each year.

Northern Hound's Tongue
Cynoglossum boreale
Boraginaceae (Borage) Family

Arching inflorescences produce 4 bristly nutlets, a trait of Hound's Tongue species. Northern Hound's Tongue has small blue flowers.

Basal leaves are broad (once thought to look like a hound's tongue). Leaves diminish in size as they progress up the stem.

Prairie Sage
Artemesia ludoviciana
Asteraceae (Aster) Family

Primarily a Western species, but has moved eastward into dryer, sunny locations of the Great Lakes region. Leaves are gray from being covered with fine hairs. A sage fragrance is emitted when the plant is crushed. Grows to 2 feet tall. Other *Artemesia* species are on pages 198 and 199.

A tall plant growing up to 3 feet, Marsh Hedge Nettle displays whorls of 6 magenta flowers at intervals along the upper part of the stem. Fine hairs cover all parts of the plant. Here, growing in a wet place, the stem has a deeper red color than the same species found growing in dryer locations.

Marsh Hedge Nettle
Stachys palustris
Lamiaceae (Mint) Family

121

Northern Bog Orchid
Platanthera hyperborea
Orchidaceae (Orchid) Family

Northern Bog Orchid, aka Northern Green Orchis, *Habenaria hyperborea* (explanation page 84), is adapted to a wide range of environments, from wet to dry, sun to shade and forest soils to bogs. This temperate climate, terrestrial orchid, stands about 3 feet tall.

Grass Pink
Calopogon pulchellus
Orchidaceae (Orchid) Family

Each plant has only one long, grass-like leaf coming from the base of the stem. Each stem supports 2 or more magenta to pink flowers. The flower is positioned to make it appear upside down with the yellow crested lip at the top or side.

Lightly shaded Sphagnum bogs and swampy areas are places to look for Grass Pinks.

Common Sow Thistle
Sonchus oleraceus
Asteraceae (Aster) Family

Sow thistles are widespread along roadsides, fields and waste places. These tall plants have stems flowing with a white milky juice which is exuded when the stem is broken.

Recurved leaf shape and spines of S. *asper* distinguish it from S. *oleraceus.*

Bright yellow, Dandelion-like flowers of both species are attention getters when in bloom.

Spiny-leaved Sow Thistle
Sonchus asper
Asteraceae (Aster) Family

Wild Parsnip
Pastinaca sativa
Apiaceae (Parsley) Family

Curled Dock
Rumex crispus
Polygonaceae (Buckwheat) Family

Large-leaved Avens
Geum macrophyllum
Rosaceae (Rose) Family

Growing in wet meadows these plants have inflorescences on open branching stems 1 to 3 foot tall. Flowers that resemble Cinquefoils mature into round, bristly, dry fruits.

On the opposite page:

Wild Parsnip has yellow-green flowers compared to several similar umbel-producing species with white flowers. Its sturdy stems grow 2 to 5 feet tall. Compound leaves have 5 to 15 sessile, toothed leaflets. Being a biennial, it produces a storage taproot during the first year of growth and in the second, it flowers.

Curled Dock has wavy leaf margins. It grows 4 to 6 feet tall. Large branched inflorescences have whorls of small green flowers. Small 3-winged, dry fruits are rusty brown when mature.

Fireweed or Great Willow Herb
Epilobium angustifolium
Onagraceae (Evening Primrose) Family

Striking magenta flowers, in a long inflorescence, bloom steadily in the summer. Red seed capsules form and persist, giving the plant a glow of color in the fall. Later, the capsules break open, releasing a myriad of seeds. Each seed has a tuft of fine hairs, allowing it to be carried away by the wind.

Black or Brown-eyed Susan
Rudbeckia hirta
Asteraceae (Aster) Family

Black-eyed Susan is a familiar plant seen along roadsides, dry fields and open woods, known by large, yellow flower heads with dark brown centers. Leaves are very hairy as are the stems which grow 1 to 3 feet tall.

Palmately compound leaves with 5 to 7 long, narrow leaflets is a trait of Sulphur Cinquefoil. Flowers are larger than most Cinquefoils, up to 1 inch in diameter. Stems are up to 2 feet tall.

With its showy yellow flowers, this attractive plant is used in garden landscapes.

Rough Fruited or Sulphur Cinquefoil
Potentilla recta
Rosaceae (Rose) Family

Crown Vetch
Coronilla varia
Fabaceae (Pea or Legume) Family

Round heads of pink and white flowers are the trademarks of Crown Vetch. Its long, compound leaves divide into many small leaflets. Rambling stems spread over large areas. This is often a plant of choice for erosion control on roadsides and ditch banks. Massive displays of pink are a showy, bloomtime by-product for travelers to enjoy.

Scentless Chamomile
Matricaria maritima
Asteraceae (Aster) Family

Thread-like leaves, flower heads up to 1 1/2 inches wide
and lack of fragrance identify this as Scentless Chamomile.
Wild Chamomile, *M. chamomilla* (not shown), has smaller
flowers and pineapple scent when the leaves are crushed.

Virginia Waterleaf
Hydrophyllum virginianum
Hydrophyllaceae (Waterleaf) Family

Leaves of Virginia Waterleaf are often mottled with irregular white spots, giving the appearance of being water stained. Pale-lavender, bell-shaped flowers hang in clusters. Stamens protruding beyond the petals give the flowers a "whiskery" look.

This woodland plant thrives in shade conditions, especially when the soil is moist and humus rich.

Pipsissewa inhabits Jack and Red Pine forests. These unique plants have whorls of dark green, leathery leaves.

Nodding, waxy, pink and white flowers hang on top of a slender stem. These beautiful flowers give way to formation of brown capsules containing seeds.

Pipsissewa
Chimaphila umbellata
Ericaceae (Heath) Family

Leaves of Wintergreen persist overwinter, becoming red-bronze in color. Red berries produced the previous summer remain all winter if not eaten by critters.

By mid-summer, the bronze leaves have been replaced by bright green leaves. White bell-shaped flowers dangle under the new leaves. In time new berries will be produced and the cycle continues.

Wintergreen
Gaultheria procumbens
Ericaceae (Heath) Family

Seed Pods

Tower Mustard
Arabis glabra
Brassicaceae (Mustard) Family

Tower Mustard has a basal rosette of slightly lobed, lance-shaped leaves. Upper leaves have lobes that clasp the stem. Purplish coloration of stem and leaves is common. Flowers vary from white to a yellow color. Long thin seed pods point upward and are held close to the stem. Plants may grow to 4 feet tall.

Yellow flower heads, like miniature Dandelions, cover the top of Canada Lettuce plants which grow 3 to 6 feet tall. Leaves are variable, some being deeply lobed and others only slightly lobed, if at all.

Like Dandelions, these seeds are tufted and blow away with the wind.

The reddish-purple stem of the plant in the photo is not necessarily typical, but may be colored due to growing conditions.

Canada Lettuce
Lactuca canadensis
Asteraceae (Aster) Family

137

Great Solomon's-seal
Polygonatum commutatum
Liliaceae (Lily) Family

Great Solomon's-seal has flower clusters of two to several per node. *P. biflorum* usually has only two flowers per node. *P. commutatum* is reported to be a tetraploid, having twice the number of chromosomes as *P. biflorum*. Some authors prefer to list these variants as a single species, *P. biflorum*.

Solomon's-seal
Polygonatum biflorum
Liliaceae (Lily) Family

Marsh or Bedstraw Bellflower
Campanula aparinoides
Campanulaceae (Bluebell) Family

Flowers, white or tinged with pale blue, grace weak stems that resemble bedstraw. Using Sensitive Fern as support, these stems are able to hang on with tiny, grasping bristles. Marsh Bellflower grows in wet, sunny meadows or bogs.

Bristly Sarsaparilla
Aralia hispida
Araliaceae (Ginsing) Family

Flower stalks branch from bristly, above-ground stems, a trait that sets this species apart from Wild Sarsaparilla on page 20. Round umbels of white flowers produce a display of blue-black berries. Bristly Sarsaparilla grows to nearly 4 feet tall in peat land and open woods.

Common Mullein
Verbascum thapsus
Scrophulariaceae (Snapdragon) Family

Wormseed Mustard
Erysimum cheiranthoides
Brassicaceae (Mustard) Family

Wormseed Mustard grows up to 3 feet tall. Leaves are long and narrow with just a few "teeth" along the edges. Long, thin seed pods, once formed, are held erect and somewhat parallel to the stem.

Mullein towers above other plants, growing to a height of 6 to 8 feet. Large velvety leaves (up to 12 inches long) and a thick, woolly stem give this plant a character all its own. Being a biennial, in its first year of growth a large rosette of basal leaves form. In the second year, the tall flower stalk is produced.

141

Marsh or Common Skullcap
Scutellaria epilobiifolia
Lamiaceae (Mint) Family

Marsh Skullcap typically has one flower in each leaf axil. With opposite leaves and flowers in each leaf axil pointing the same direction, the flowers appear to be "twins" arising from the same node.

As the name indicates, wet places like marshes, lake shores and swampy meadows are places to look for this plant. It grows 1 to 3 feet tall.

Yellow Fringed Orchid
Platanthera ciliaris
Orchidaceae (Orchid) Family

Downy Rattlesnake Plantain
Goodyera pubescens
Orchidaceae (Orchid) Family

The distinct netted pattern of the leaves and white midrib band are standard clues to identification of *G. pubescens*. Deciduous forests with acidic soil is its preferred habitat.

Yellow Fringed Orchid is seldom seen. Its range is in the Eastern part of the Great Lakes region. Very rare today, it is listed as endangered in several states. On the positive side, research is being conducted in order to propagate and to reintroduce this lovely Orchid back into the wild.

The "fringes" of Fringed Loosestrife are on the upper edge of leaf petioles.

Nodding yellow flowers have contrasting bright red-orange eyes and tiny "teeth" at the tips of the petals.

Plants grow 1 to 3 feet tall in a range of moist habitats.

Fringed Loosestrife
Lysimachia ciliata
Primulaceae
    (Primrose) Family

Swamp Candles
Lysimachia terrestris
Primulaceae (Primrose) Family

Shaded by a tree on a lake shore, Swamp Candle is in a typical habitat. These plants, with terminal flower clusters, grow about 2 feet tall.

Marsh Cinquefoil has large red sepals longer than smaller red petals. Together the petals and sepals form flowers about one inch in diameter.

Stems up to 2 feet long tend to be sprawling in their wet bog or swamp habitats.

Marsh Cinquefoil
Potentilla palustris
Rosaceae (Rose) Family

Woolly Yarrow
Achillea lanulosa
Asteraceae (Aster) Family

Woolly Yarrow stems and leaves are densely covered with matted pubescense making them look dark gray.

A. lanulosa is native to the western part of the Great Lakes region. A similar species, Common Yarrow (*A. millefolium* of European origin), has also naturalized throughout the region.

Both species have finely divided leaves often described as fern-like, but Common Yarrow is not woolly.

Common Agrimony
Agrimonia gryposepala
Rosaceae (Rose) Family

From a distance, Agrimony inflorescences can be mistaken for Yellow Sweet Clover, but their flowers are definitely different. A closer look reveals tiny 5-petaled, radial, yellow flowers typical of the Rose Family. The leaves of Agrimony are compound with several leaflets. The fruits have hooked prickles which stick tightly to clothing and animal fur.

Evening Primrose
Oenothera biennis.
Onagraceae (Evening Primrose) Family

These flowers will open wide in the evening, revealing 4 large petals, each up to one inch long. Evening Primrose may grow up to 6 feet high.

Erigeron species, called Fleabanes, are aster-like plants that usually bloom earlier than Asters. Ray flowers are more numerous in Fleabanes. *E. strigosus* has 50 to 100 rays which are white. Central disk flowers are yellow. Compare *E. philadelphicus,* page 117.

Lesser Daisy Fleabane
Erigeron strigosus
Asteraceae (Aster) Family

Pink petals dotted with white and having "teeth" on the edges are clues for recognizing Deptford Pink. Long narrow leaves grow on a slender stem, 12 to 18 inches tall. Its grassy habitat makes it a natural along roadsides, meadows and clearings in woods.

Notches at the petal tips are a trait of the Pink Family. Some petals look like they have been trimmed with pinking shears, and so are called "pinks." Pinks come in a variety of colors.

Deptford Pink
Dianthus armeria
Caryophyllaceae (Pink) Family

One Bloom at a Time

Round-leaved Sundew
Drosera rotundifolia
Droseraceae (Sundew) Family

Sundew plants are carnivorous. In the nutrient-poor Sphagnum bog, Sundew leaves are adapted for catching insects. Trapped insects, a good nitrogen source, are digested and their nutrients are absorbed into the plant's system. Spoon-shaped leaves, attractively colored, have many glandular hairs that secrete sweet droplets at their tips as "bait" for the insects.

Nodding Flower Stalk

Can you find the Sundew? This tiny plant brings us to our knees!

Searching on hands and knees in Sphagnum Moss bogs is necessary to closely observe these colorful, delicate plants. Sundew leaves, only 1 to 3 inches long, grow in a rosette. A single, nodding flower stalk arises from the center. Flowers bloom one at a time starting with the lowest bud and continuing to the top of the stalk.

Dark dots on otherwise clear yellow petals and conspicuous stamens are natural characteristics of St. John's Wort.

Narrow, oblong, oppositely arranged, sessile leaves are attached to the main stem and branches.

This *Hypericum* is a common weed along roadsides and open fields, growing more than 2 feet tall.

Common St. John's Wort
Hypericum perforatum
Hypericaceae
      (St. John's Wort) Family

Thimbleweed is also called Tall Anemone. It grows to up to 3 feet in height. Flower centers appear as "buttons" which stretch as they develop into "thimbles." Each long flower stalk supports one flower made up of 5 white petal-like sepals.

Thimbleweed
Anemone virginiana
Ranunculaceae (Buttercup) Family

Blooms of Goldenrods seem to mark the transition to late summer. Various species come into bloom throughout the remainder of the growing season.

Goldenrod species are numerous; over 60 are listed in taxonomy books for this region. Many of the species are so similar they are difficult to identify. Flower head "forms" characterize general groups of Goldenrods. These forms include plume-like, elm-branched, club-like, wand-like and flat-topped.

Early Goldenrod
Solidago juncea
Asteraceae (Aster) Family

Early Goldenrod is described as plume-like. Basal leaves are broad and toothed, but leaves on the upper part of the stem are narrow and entire.

Swamp Smartweed
Polygonum coccineum
Polygonaceae (Buckwheat) Family

Like Water Smartweed, (page 159), Swamp Smartweed has an aquatic and terrestrial form as shown here. In this terrestrial habitat, Swamp Smartweed has an erect form. Inflorescences are longer in *P. coccineum* than in *P. amphibium.*

Common or Broadleaf Arrowhead
Sagittaria latifolia
Alismataceae (Arrowhead) Family

Leaves of Common Arrowhead are arrow-shaped and can have very narrow to broad lobes. Flowers are in whorls of 3, and each flower has 3 white petals. Quiet, shallow water of ponds, lake shores and slow-moving streams provide habitat.

Water Smartweed
Polygonum amphibium
Polygonaceae
(Buckwheat) Family

Water Smartweed is similar to Swamp Smartweed (page 157). Both have aquatic and terrestrial forms. Here the aquatic form of *P. amphibium* is growing in typical habitat. Note the flower stalks are held above the water with a pink cluster of flowers being about 1 1/2 inches long.

Floating leaves of Water Smartweed are broader and more blunt on the tip than the terrestrial form.

Blooming later than other *Pyrola* species (page 87), Shinleaf grows through the mulch of pine forests.

Leaves of Shinleaf are large, egg-shaped and not as thick or leathery as other *Pyrola*.

White flowers bloom on slender 6 to 10 inch stalks.

Shinleaf
Pyrola elliptica
Pyrolaceae (Wintergreen) Family

Common Speedwell
Veronica officinalis
Scrophulariaceae (Snapdragon) Family

Common Speedwell has hairy, trailing stems with finely-toothed, egg-shaped leaves. Dainty lavender flowers have 4 petals. A trait of *Veronica* shows 3 similar sized petals and one, the lower petal, being decidedly smaller.

Selections of Clustered Bellflower are extensively used in home landscapes. It is an alien that has escaped into natural areas and along roadsides. Plants grow 1 to 2 feet tall and produce an attractive tight cluster of blue flowers at the tip of the stem.

Clustered Bellflower
Campanula glomerata
Campanulaceae (Blubell) Family

Small, four-petaled pink flowers are deeply notched at the tip of each petal. Notched petal tips are displayed by many species, but it is a specific trait of the Pink Family. Pink Family flowers usually have 5 petals.

Plants grow 1 to 3 feet tall and have shiny green leaves that are edged with shallow teeth.

Seeds with whitish hairs are produced in long, brown seed pods.

Northern Willow Herb
Epilobium glandulosum
Onagraceae (Evening Primrose) Family

Wild Mint
Mentha arvensis
Lamiaceae (Mint) Family

Wild Mint has lavender (and occasionally white) flowers tightly clustered in its leaf axils. Leaves are oblong, serrated and have a strong mint smell when crushed. Hairy stems grow 1 to 2 feet tall, usually in moist open places, but sometimes in dry locations.

Spotted Joe Pye Weed is another name given this plant because its stem may be purple-spotted rather than solid purple.

Toothed leaves are in whorls of 4 or 5 on a stem 3 to 5 feet tall.

As flower buds open, the inflorescence becomes more flattened on top and is covered with small, fuzzy-looking pink flowers.

A native plant, Joe Pye Weed has made its way into home gardens and landscapes where tall plants are desired.

Joe Pye Weed
Eupatorium maculatum
Asteraceae (Aster) Family

Queen Anne's Lace is Wild Carrot. A rosette of finely divided leaves and a fleshy root similar to the roots and leaves of garden variety carrots marks the first year of growth. In the second year, a long stem up to 3 or 4 feet is topped with a flat umbel of tiny white flowers. Stiff, 3-forked bracts under the umbel separate this plant from other white flowered, umbel-producing species.

Queen Anne's Lace
Daucus carota
Apiaceae (Parsley) Family

Flowers of Pearly Everlasting are in rounded heads that have many dry, white, petal-like bracts surrounding yellow disk flowers. Male and female flowers are produced on separate plants.

Stems growing 1 to 3 feet tall are woolly and have long narrow leaves which are also woolly on the underside.

Dry, open places are preferred habitat, but Pearly Everlasting also grows in light-shaded forest edges.

Pearly Everlasting
Anaphalis margaritacea
Asteraceae (Aster) Family

Growing in diverse habitats, Purple Fringed Orchid may be found in shade or full sunlight, in organic or mineral soils, in wet woods or in meadows.

Its stem grows up to 3 feet high including the inflorescence.

Purple Fringed Orchid's scientific name is also listed as *Habenaria psycodes* in many references (explanation on page 84).

Purple Fringed Orchid
Platanthera psycodes
Orchidaceae (Orchid) Family

Water Plantain
Alisma triviale
Alismataceae (Arrowhead) Family

White, 3-petaled flowers of Water Plantain are usually borne in whorls of 4. Branched flower stalks arise from a circular base of upright, elliptical leaves. These plants typically grow in shallow water or muddy ditches or edges of ponds.

A similar species *A. subcordatum*, Small Water Plantain (not shown), has smaller flowers with petals no longer in length than the green sepals.

169

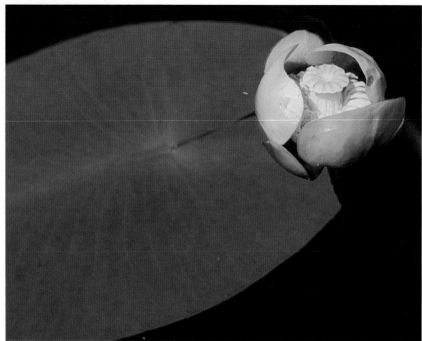

A plant of many names, Yellow Water Lily is known as Bullhead Lily, Spatterdock, Pond Lily and Cow Lily. By whatever name, it is common to many lakes, quiet streams and ponds throughout the region.

Large floating leaves up to 12 inches long grow from a submerged rhizome.

Yellow Water Lily
Nuphar variegatum
Nymphaeaceae (Water Lily) Family

Flowers have a whorl of 5 or 6 yellow or yellow-green sepals that resemble fleshy petals. Many small petals that look like stamens are inside the large, cup-shaped sepals. The center of the flower has a stigma that looks like a "toadstool." This unusual flower is held above the water on its own thick stalk.

Fragrant Water Lily, also called Sweet Scented Water Lily, displays showy white petals.

Round floating leaves are usually purplish underneath.

A similar lily, White or Tuberous Water Lily (*N. tuberosa)* does not have fragrance, and its leaves are green on the under-side.

Fragrant Water Lily
Nymphaea odorata
Nymphaeaceae (Water Lily) Family

Standing as much as 3 to 4 feet tall in wet marshes or lake shores, Swamp Milkweed blooms with a striking cluster of rose-purple flowers. Unique milkweed flower structure is evident, shown by downward-pointing petals in the photo below.

Above the petals are 5 erect hoods, each having a curved crest pointing inward. At the flower's center is a white stigma.

Swamp Milkweed
Asclepias incarnata
Asclepiadaceae (Milkweed) Family

Purple Loosestrife has a dense spike of purple to pink flowers on 2 to 4 foot stems. A handsome plant, once considered choice for home gardens, it is now listed as a noxious weed in many areas. When established in swamps and marshes, it grows rampantly, crowding out native plants.

Purple Loosestrife
Lythrum salicaria
Lythraceae (Loosestrife) Family

173

Stems of Rough Bedstraw are square, weak and somewhat prickly (rough to the touch). Leaves less than 1 inch long are usually in whorls of 6, but sometimes there are 4 or 5 in a whorl.

Small white flowers are abundant.

Cleavers, *G. aparine* (not pictured), is similar in appearance except it has bigger leaves 1 to 3 inches long.

Rough Bedstraw
Galium asprellum
Rubiaceae (Bedstraw) Family

Blue Vervain flower clusters are slender spikes having only a few lavender-blue flowers open at one time.

Stems grow 2 to 5 feet tall with opposite, coarsely-toothed leaves. Lower leaves are sometimes lobed.

It grows in dry and open habitats.

Blue Vervain
Verbena hastata
Verbenaceae (Vervain) Family

Butter-and-Eggs
Linaria vulgaris
Scrophulariaceae (Snapdragon) Family

Bi-colored yellow and orange flowers grow on a spike-like stalk up to 3 feet tall.

Gardeners, delighted with their pretty Snapdragon-like blossoms, brought them to America from Europe. Beauty is only blossom deep, for it spreads rapidly in a garden and on to any dry, sunny location where soil has been disturbed. Unfortunately, Butter and Eggs is a pesky weed.

Tall Sunflower is a perennial that thrives in wet places. Its alternate, lance-shaped leaves are rough with little or no stalk attaching them to the reddish-colored, 4 to 10 foot stem.

Among the many sunflower species in this region, all have similar characteristics. Commercially grown sunflowers have been developed by selecting and breeding desirable traits, especially those of *H. annuus*, one of the wild sunflowers.

Tall or Giant Sunflower
Helianthus giganteus
Asteraceae (Aster) Family

Jewelweed or
Spotted Touch-me-not
Impatiens capensis
Balsaminaceae
(Touch-me-not) Family

This annual plant is closely related to the popular tropical *Impatiens* raised extensively as bedding plants in shady landscapes. A native of the temperate climate, Jewelweed thrives in wet, shady places.

Jewelweed stems, about 2 to 5 feet tall, are hollow and succulent, but support orange-spotted yellow flowers as they dangle from long stalks.

Seed capsules, about 1 inch long, become plump when ripe and "explode" on contact with anything that touches them. The force twists the capsule inside out. Note the immature capsule (left) and spent capsule being held by the photographer.

Hoary Alyssum grows about 1 to 2 feet tall. Lance-shaped leaves are grayish due to a downy covering.

Flowers have 4 deeply cleft petals thickly clustered on a flower stalk that continues to elongate. The result is a long stalk with flattened oval seed capsules along its side.

Hoary Alyssum
Berteroa incana
Brassicaceae (Mustard) Family

Harebell
Campanula rotundifolia
Campanulaceae (Bluebell) Family

Harebell seems to grow in some of the most inhospitable places imaginable, such as this rocky ledge along Lake Superior's north shore. Thin wiry stems, rarely over 15 inches tall, have fine leaves and delicate, bell-shaped flowers.

Creeping Bellflower, also called European Bellflower, is a robust plant growing to 1 to 3 feet tall. It forms large patches on roadsides and open areas, propagating by spreading rootstocks as well as by seed dispersal.

Nodding, blue, bell-shaped flowers over 1 inch in length develop on just one side of the flower stalk.

Creeping Bellflower
Campanula rapunculoides
Campanulaceae (Bluebell) Family

Flowers of Canada Thistle are pretty, but oh, those prickly leaves!

Underground stems (rhizomes) provide the invading process of this plant, making it hard to eradicate once established. Grows 1 to 3 feet tall.

Canada Thistle
Cirsium arvense
Asteraceae (Aster) Family

Bull Thistle
Cirsium vulgare
Asteraceae (Aster) Family

A giant among thistles, Bull Thistle lives up to its name: One doesn't toy with this plant. Armed with sharp, prickly leaves and stems, Bull Thistle needs careful handling. A single plant can grow up to 6 feet tall and 3 feet wide.

Enchanter's Nightshade
Circaea quadrisulcata
Onagraceae (Evening Primrose) Family

Innocent-looking, delicate white flowers, clearly notched at the tip of each petal, bloom in loose clusters. The flowers seem inviting but with time, pear-shaped fruits covered with hooked bristles develop. These tiny bristles cling tightly to clothing and fur, making the fruits difficult to remove.

Leaves are opposite and elliptical. Lower leaves have long petioles, but those higher on the stem are nearly sessile.

Turtlehead
Chelone glabra
Scrophulariaceae (Snapdragon) Family

Turtlehead thrives in damp places, growing up to 3 feet tall. Flowers of *C. glabra* are about 1 inch long and have an arched upper lip that resembles a turtle's head. Leaves are opposite, lance-shaped and have fine serrations.

Other Turtlehead species *C. lyoni* (pink) and *C. obliqua* (red), are not as prevalent in this region, but are chosen along with *C. glabra* as landscape plants for their lovely fall bloom.

185

Queen of the Meadow
Filipendula ulmaria
Rosaceae (Rose) Family

Looking like wisps of clouds, Queen of the Meadow flowers atop 4 foot stems make this plant an attractive ornamental for home gardens. A garden escapee, it has naturalized and grows in roadside ditches and meadows.

A similar pink-flowered species, Queen of the Prairie, *F. rubra*, is more common in southerly regions.

Day Lily flowers are without spots as compared to other wild lilies of the region (pages 96, 114, 115, 189)

Long grass-like leaves form clumps. Leaves and flower stalks of Day Lily arise from the crown of the plant at ground level. In the photo bottom right, Day Lily foliage makes a good backdrop for the Geranium in bloom. Soon the Day Lily will come into its own bloom-time.

Originally from Japan, *H. fulva* was brought to North America as a horticultural garden plant. It is now widely naturalized.

Hemerocallis species have pleased gardeners for generations. Today there are hundreds of beautiful cultivars that have been produced and are commercially available.

Day Lily
Hemerocallis fulva
Liliaceae (Lily) Family

Common Tansy
Tanacetum vulgare
Asteraceae (Aster) Family

Tansy, once favored as a garden flower, has become a weed, spreading over roadsides, vacant lots, open fields and waste places. It forms large patches. Finely divided leaves release fragrance when crushed. Button-like, yellow flower heads form flat-topped inflorescences.

Tiger Lily
Lilium tigrinum
Liliaceae (Lily) Family

Like Turk's Cap and Michigan Lilies on pages 114 and 115, Tiger Lily has orange, nodding, spotted flowers. However, *L. tigrinum* can be distinguished by purple stems, alternately arranged leaves, and little bulblets in the leaf axils on the upper part of the stem.

Nipplewort
Lapsana communis
Asteraceae (Aster) Family

Petite flower heads of a soft yellow color are only half an inch across and bloom on stiff, slender, branched stems. Stems grow up to 3 feet tall. Egg-shaped leaves are slightly toothed and may be lobed on the lower portion of the stem.

Common Burdock
Arctium minus
Asteraceae (Aster) Family

Attractive pink but bristly flower heads of Burdock ripen into clinging burs.

Oval leaves are alternately arranged on a thick, grooved and hollow stem growing up to 5 feet tall.

Only a basal rosette of leaves forms the first season, but this clump may be up to 3 feet in diameter. Like a true biennial, the second season's growth produces the flower stalk.

Hemp Nettle
Galeopsis tetrahit
Lamiaceae (Mint) Family

Hemp Nettle has two-lipped flowers, the upper lip projecting over the opening and the 3 lobed lower lip having two prominent "nipples" projecting upward at its base. Flowers are up to three-fourths inch long.

Bristly stems bear oval, coarsely-toothed leaves that resemble those of Stinging Nettle (page 220), but there are no stinging hairs on Hemp Nettle leaves.

Diminutive white flowers appearing on slender spikes identifies White Vervain. Leaves are opposite and coarsely serrated. White Vervain grows 3 to 5 feet tall on stems that are usually hairy.

White Vervain
Verbena urticifolia
Verbenaceae (Vervain) Family

193

White Lettuce Flowers

White Lettuce with Triangular Leaves   Brownish Pappus Under Sepals

194

White Lettuce Flowers (pink form)

White Lettuce is one of a group of plants called Rattlesnake Root. Others include Tall Rattlesnake Root *(P. trifoliata)*, Lion's Foot *(P. serpentaria)* and Boott's Rattlesnake Root *(P. bootii)*. All of these species have leaves that vary widely in structure, a curious growth habit.

In White Lettuce, leaves vary from triangular shape on the plant pictured on the facing page to the deeply lobed leaves shown right. Stems are usually purple growing 2 to 5 feet tall.

Flowers of White Lettuce are identified with the brownish colored hairs beneath the sepals called the pappus. Flower color may range from white to pinkish.

White Lettuce
Prenanthes alba
Asteraceae (Aster) Family

Indentations at the petal tips identify this as Musk Mallow along with
leaves divided into narrow segments.
Flowers may be white as well as
pink with many stamens fused to a
central pistil, a characteristic of the
Mallow Family.

These plants, escaped from cultivation, are found along roadsides and
waste places.

Musk Mallow
Malva moschata
Malvaceae (Mallow) Family

Horseweed
Erigeron canadensis
Asteraceae (Aster) Family

Flowers of Horseweed are in tiny heads about one-eighth inch long. These heads remain tightly closed until small tufted seeds form and are released to be scattered by the wind. Narrow, lance-shaped leaves are on hairy stems. Plants may be as much as 7 feet tall.

197

Wormwood and Mugwort are names applied to several *Artemisia* species, creating certain confusion about plant identity. Dry, sandy areas, including beaches and dunes of the Great Lakes, are likely habitats.

Tall Wormwood, *A. caudata*, has very finely divided and forked, silvery-colored leaves. Numerous, small, nodding flower heads line up on long stalks. Red stems to 2 feet tall are characteristic of this *Artemisia*. Prairie Sage on page 120 is another *Artemisia*.

Tall Wormwood
Artemisia caudata
Asteraceae (Aster) Family

Absinthe Wormwood
Artemisia absinthium
Asteraceae (Aster) Family

Gray-green, drooping flower heads of Absinthe Wormwood are larger than those of Tall Wormwood. Leaves are deeply cut on the lower part of the stem, becoming progressively smaller on the upper portion of the plant.

Dense rounded heads of pinkish to pale lavender flowers top square, erect stems 2 to 3 feet tall. Bees commonly visit these flowers for the nectar used in honey production.

Other species of Bergamot in the region include Bee Balm or Oswego Tea *(M. didyma)* and Purple Bergamot *(M. media)*.

Colorful hybrid cultivars have been produced for landscape use.

Wild Bergamot
Monarda fistulosa
Lamiaceae (Mint) Family

Gray Headed Coneflower
Ratibida pinnata
Asteraceae (Aster) Family

Long yellow ray flowers droop downward in *R. pinnata,* and the central disk (seed producing) flowers are on a long "cone."

Leaves are deeply cut into 3 to 7 narrow, toothed segments. A hairy stem grows 3 to 5 feet tall.

Dry meadows and roadsides are natural habitats for Gray Headed Coneflower.

Gray Goldenrod
Solidago nemoralis
Asteraceae (Aster) Family

Gray Goldenrod has "plume-like" inflorescences. Short stems, 10 to 24 inches. Narrow leaves are fuzzy, giving them a gray-green color. Tiny leaflets grow out of the leaf axils.

Showy Goldenrod
Solidago speciosa
Asteraceae (Aster) Family

Flower clusters point upward in Showy Goldenrod, a "club-like" type. Flowers on the lower part of the stem develop later than terminal ones. The inflorescence widens at the bottom.

Greater or Late Goldenrod
Solidago gigantea
Asteraceae (Aster) Family

Goldenrod's gentle giant, *S. gigantea*, grows up to 7 feet tall topped with a large plume-like inflorescence. Stems may be green or purplish. Leaves are sharply toothed and lance-shaped. Greater Goldenrod thrives in both moist and dry places.

Goldenrod Trivia

Goldenrod pollen has been berated as the culprit for causing hay fever. Goldenrods are insect pollinated. This pollen does not readily become wind borne. However the real culprit is another Aster Family plant, Common Ragweed (page 213). Its pollen is wind blown and does cause allergic reactions.

Galls often form on Goldenrod stems (below). Insect larvae grow inside the stem, forming the enlargement. *S. gigantea* and *S. canadensis* are prone to this kind of invasion.

Taxonomists have identified over 60 species of Goldenrod in Northeast United States and adjacent Canada. Species are hard to identify: Minute characteristics must be used to classify them. To complicate the identities even more, hybridization between species may occur.

Prairie or Missouri Goldenrod
Solidago missouriensis
Asteraceae (Aster) Family

Open, drooping branches of flower heads identify "elm-branched" types of Goldenrod. Clues to Prairie Goldenrod are smooth, lance-shaped leaves, mostly with 3 "nerves" (major veins); lower leaves may have serrations. Stems are smooth and hairless and grow up to 3 feet tall.

Lance or Grass-leaved Goldenrod
Euthamia (Solidago) graminifolia
Asteraceae (Aster) Family

Narrow, lance-shaped leaves and a "flat-topped" inflorescence type identify this Goldenrod. It grows 2 to 4 feet tall in moist or dry places. Older references list this in genus *Solidago*.

A thick, flat cluster of white flower heads (each with only 7 to 14 ray flowers and yellow disk flowers in the center of each inflorescence) describes Flat-topped Aster. It has lance-shaped, entire leaves on a stem reaching up to 7 feet high.

Flat-topped Aster
Aster umbellatus
Asteraceae (Aster) Family

Large-leaved Aster
Aster macrophyllus
Asteraceae (Aster) Family

Large-leaved Aster is easy to recognize by its huge basal leaves which reach 4 to 8 inches wide. Many deciduous forest floors become covered with this Aster in the springtime (right).

Upper leaves are smaller and sessile. Disk flowers are yellow while ray flowers are lavender and number about 10 to 20.

Lowrie's Aster
Aster lowrieanus
Asteraceae (Aster) Family

Lowrie's Aster, with a distinctive heart-shaped leaf, has a flat, winged petiole (photo lower right). Purplish stems are common. Flower heads with 8 to 20 lavender rays are arranged in long, open panicles.

Calico, Necklace or Side-flowering Aster
Aster lateriflorus
Asteraceae (Aster) Family

White or purple-tinged ray flowers surround a purple disk on *A. lateriflorus*. These small flower heads tend to be on one side of the flower stalk.

Spotted Knapweed
Centaurea maculosa
Asteraceae (Aster) Family

Spotted Knapweed has gray-colored, deeply-cut leaves and pink to purple thistle-like flowers. Much branched, stiff stems give the plant an "open" appearance. The "spot" of Spotted Knapweed comes from a black tip on the bracts surrounding the flower heads.

Most Parsley Family plants have flat-topped umbels, but Rattlesnake Master has a round, tight flower cluster. These flowers are small and white. Stiff, Yucca-like leaves with spiny edges can grow to 3 feet long. Over all, Rattlesnake Master may reach 4 feet in height.

Rattlesnake Master
Eryngium yuccifolium
Apiaceae (Parsley) Family

212

Common Ragweed
Ambrosia artemisiifolia
Asteraceae (Aster) Family

A slender spike-like inflorescence, 3 to 5 inches long, carries tiny green flowers, the culprits that discharge hay-fever-inducing pollen into the air. Leaves are finely divided into numerous segments. Plants may grow up to 6 feet tall.

Look for Chicory in the morning. By afternoon, the flowers have closed for the day!

Flower heads with striking blue rays grace Chicory plants on the roadside (opposite page). Each flower ray has a conspicuous serrated tip (below). Flower heads may reach 1.5 inches in diameter.

Dried roots are roasted and ground to flavor coffee or used as a coffee substitute. Dandelion-like basal leaves can be gathered in the spring when they are tender and used as salad greens.

Chicory
Cichorium intybus
Asteraceae (Aster) Family

215

Double Flower Form

Single Flower Form

Bouncing Bet or Soapwort
Saponaria officinalis
Caryophyllaceae (Pink) Family

Bouncing Bet may have single or double flowers, either pink or white. Wort means plant; soapwort translates "soap plant." The presence of saponin produces soap-like suds. Pioneers used this plant as a detergent.

Pennsylvania Smartweed
Polygonum pensylvanicum
Polygonaceae (Buckwheat) Family

Pennsylvania Smartweed flowers, rose to white, line spike-like inflorescences. Leaves are smooth, entire and lance-shaped on reddish stems. This color is especially pronounced at leaf nodes. Similar species in the region, *P. lapathifolium*, Pale or Nodding Smartweed, has a green stem. *P. persicaria*, Lady's Thumb, usually exhibits a dark blotch on its leaves.

Pale Corydalis
Corydalis sempervirens
Papaveraceae Poppy) Family

In close-up or in mass, these pink flowers with yellow tips
are handsome. Attractive lobed, pale-green leaves grow on
branched stems. Pale Corydalis plants reach 2 feet in height.
Slender seed capsules produce many, many tiny black seeds.
Compare Yellow Corydalis on page 10.

Purple Giant Hyssop
Agastache scrophulariaefolia
Lamiaceae (Mint) Family

Lavender-purple flowers circle a crowded spike. Coarsely-toothed leaves have a hairy, white underside. Stems are reddish in color and grow 2 to 5 feet tall.

Slender Nettle
Urtica gracilis
Urticaceae (Nettle) Family

Slender Nettle resembles its close relative, the notorius Stinging Nettle *(U. dioica)*. An encounter with Stinging Nettle is one to be avoided! Tiny stinging hairs cover the leaves and stems. Any touch on bare skin could produce a painful dermatitis. Slender Nettle has fewer stinging hairs and narrower lance-shaped leaves.

String-like clusters of diminuitive greenish flowers hang from the leaf axils. Leaves are lance-shaped and moderately serrated. Stinging Nettle leaves are broader and heart-shaped. Plants grow 3 to 5 feet tall.

Indian Pipe
Monotropa uniflora
Pyrolaceae (Wintergreen) Family

Indian Pipe thrives in dense shade of moist woodlands. It doesn't have green chlorophyll, therefore it doesn't need light for photosynthesis. A symbiotic relationship exists with other organisms. Food is absorbed from hosts (other green plants or fungi). Like Coral Root (page 40), it is a flowering, seed producing plant. The photos above illustrate flower buds pointed upward and about to open. Flowers are white. Upon opening, they bend downward to form a "pipe." Scale-like leaves are small and turn brown as the plant ages. White stems grow 4 to 8 inches tall.

White Aster
Aster spp.
Asteraceae (Aster) Family

Asters rival Goldenrod for number of species in the region, with over 60 being identified and described.

As a matter of course, Asters commonly hybridize, producing intermediate forms which makes their identification even more confusing!

Blue Aster
Aster spp.
Asteraceae (Aster) Family

Small groups of flower heads alternate from side to side at the base of oval leaves giving this Goldenrod stem a "zig-zag" appearance. Thriving in woodland habitats, plants grow up to 3 feet in height.

Zig-zag Goldenrod
Solidago flexicaulis
Asteraceae (Aster) Family

Located in a "flat top" cluster, flower heads of Stiff Goldenrod are larger than most other Goldenrods. Stems grow up to 5 feet tall and carry broad leaves that are thick, having a cardboard-like texture.

Hard-leaved or Stiff Goldenrod
Solidago rigida
Asteraceae (Aster) Family

Commonly seen on roadsides, meadows and open areas, Canada Goldenrod exhibits "plume-like" clusters on the tips of stems up to 4 feet tall. Leaves are long, narrow and sharply toothed.

Canada Goldenrod
Solidago canadensis
Asteraceae (Aster) Family

Canada Hawkweed is identified by the toothed, sessile leaves ascending the stem to the floral branches. Stems may grow over 4 feet tall. Flower heads are about 1 inch in diameter.

Canada Hawkweed
Hieracium canadense
Asteraceae (Aster) Family

Spurred Gentian
Halenia deflexa
Gentianaceae
(Gentian) Family

Greenish-colored Spurred Gentian flowers have 4 fused petals with "spurs" pointing downward. Broad leaves are sessile. It only grows about 1 to 2 feet in height. Trail sides and edges of moist woodlands are typical habitats.

Closed or Bottle Gentian
Gentiana andrewsii
Gentianaceae (Gentian) Family

Bright blue flowers never open on Closed Gentian. Sessile, oval leaves taper to a point on stems about 1 to 2 feet in height. Habitats are similar to Spurred Gentian.

Bugleweeds are mint-like plants in general characteristics, but their leaves do not emit a minty scent. White flowers gather tightly in the leaf axils. Notice the coarsely toothed leaf edges. Leaves taper to a long narrow point on Northern Bugleweed.

Lycopus species (not shown) differ slightly: *L. virginicus*, Virginia Bugleweed, leaves are broader, more oval. *L. americanus*, Cut-leaved or Common Water Horehound, has leaves that are more deeply cut or nearly lobed.

Northern Bugleweed
Lycopus uniflorus
Lamiaceae (Mint) Family

Pointed-leaved Tick-trefoil
Desmodium glutinosum
Fabaceae (Pea) Family

A long, slender, branched flower stalk rising from a short stem above a whorl of leaves is a key identifying characteristic of Pointed-leaved Tick-trefoil. Pink to purplish pea-like flowers produce lobed pods covered with hooked hairs. When mature these hairy pods cling to clothing and fur.

Notice how the base of small, light blue or white flowers becomes "inflated" as the plant matures. This is an annual plant reproducing from seed and is reported to be the most common of all *Lobelia* species in this region. Moist, open areas are usual habitat.

Indian Tobacco
Lobelia inflata
Campanulaceae (Bluebell) Family

Ditch Stonecrop
Penthorum sedoides
Saxifragaceae (Saxifrage) Family

At first sight, the leaves of this plant may look like Slender Nettle (page 220). In fact, there are no stinging hairs on Ditch Stonecrop. Greenish-yellow flower clusters branch at the top of the plant. It grows 2 to 3 feet tall in wet places. Some taxonomists place *Penthorum* in the *Crassulaceae* (Sedum) Family.

Fruit of the Bloom

Goldenrod in Fall

Fall brings "harvest" and an ending to the growing season in North Country climates. Leaves turn color, wither and fall to the ground. Plants finish one more cycle of growth, flowering and forming fruit and seed. Fruits, small or large, dry and papery or soft and juicy, contain next years supply of seeds waiting to germinate in the spring. Carried by wind, water, birds or other animals, seeds are "planted" somewhere else, to begin again nature's cycle of life.

Blue Cohosh
Caulophyllum thalictroides
Berberidaceae (Barberry) Family

After initial springtime growth, greenish-yellow flowers mature into bright blue fruits. Blue Cohosh is much easier to recognize in the fall. Although the fruits resemble "blueberries" (page 250), Cohosh berries are toxic. Blue Cohosh grows in moist, nutrient rich woodlands, reaching heights of 1 to 3 feet.

Ginseng
Panax quinquefolius
Araliaceae (Ginseng) Family

Ginseng begins its spring growth with an inconspicuous round cluster of yellow-green flowers blooming on short stalks at the terminal point of the stem. Three long stalked leaves, each with 5 leaflets, also arise from the same terminal point. In the fall, berries turn bright red and remain upright in the center of the three leaves. Wild Ginseng has become a cultivated crop primarily for herbal remedies and is quite rare in its natural habitats.

Spikenard
Aralia racemosa
Araliaceae (Ginseng) Family

Imagine this cluster of purple berries starting its seed-producing cycle in late spring as hardly noticeable greenish-white flowers. Stems grow 3 to 6 feet tall and have large, spreading compound leaves with many oval leaflets. It grows well in humus-rich woodlands.

Orange fruits circle each node, having developed from dull-red, stalkless flowers.

A similar plant, Wild Coffee, *T. perfoliatum* (not shown), has leaves that are joined at the base surrounding the stem. Orange-fruited Horse Gentian leaves are sessile to the stem.

Orange-fruited Horse Gentian
Triosteum aurantiacum
Caprifoliaceae (Honeysuckle) Family

Bristly Greenbrier
Smilax hispida
Liliaceae (Lily) Family

Greenbriers are woody monocot vines. Many *Smilax* species are similar, most having thorns. Bristly Greenbrier is especially thorny. Umbels of small, greenish flowers appear in spring. Blue-black fruits develop over summer.

Vines

Plants with stems too weak to stay upright by themselves use other strategies to bring their leaves to the sunshine. Vines attach themselves either by tendrils which are modified leaves, or by winding their entire stem around supporting objects.

Carrion Flower
Smilax herbacea
Liliaceae (Lily) Family

Carrion Flower is an herbaceous vine not having a woody stem. A whiff of the flowers explains its name! Look for this plant in moist woods.

Purple Virgin's Bower is a beautiful flowering vine. Its short bloom period is in early spring, making it easy to miss.

In autumn, a showy display of feathery seed heads decorates the landscape.

Another Virgin's Bower, *C. virginiana* (page 248) blooms later.

Having showy sepals rather than petals, Virgin's Bower is a good example of this Buttercup Family characteristic.

Purple Virgin's Bower
Clematis verticillaris
Ranunculaceae (Buttercup) Family

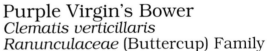

Fringed Bindweed
Polygonum cilinode
Polygonaceae (Buckwheat) Family

Loose, airy inflorescences of dainty white
flowers are prolific on sprawling stems.
These vines will cover shrubs, brush piles,
rocks or fences. Each heart-shaped leaf has
a fringed sheath surrounding the reddish
stem.

Hairy Honeysuckle
Lonicera hirsuta
Caprifoliaceae (Honeysuckle) Family

Yellow to orange flowers of Hairy Honeysuckle cluster in a circular leaf collar. These flowers produce green fruits which ripen bright red.

Hedge Bindweed
Convolvulus sepium

Upright Bindweed
Convolvulus spithamaeus

Both of these Bindweeds belong to the *Convolvu-laceae* (Morning Glory) Family. Hedge Bindweed has a long trailing stem with arrowhead-shaped leaves. Upright Bindweed stems are short (6 to 12 inches) and has elliptical leaves.

Bittersweet Nightshade is a perennial vine with weak stems that is an intrusive weed. It is recognized as being in the tomato family with its yellow "beak" of anthers and lavender petals swept backward. Bright red fruits hang in clusters all along the vine in late summer. These fruits have toxic substances and should not be eaten.

Bittersweet Nightshade
Solanum dulcamara
Solanaceae (Tomato) Family

Wild Yam
Dioscorea Villosa
Dioscoreaceae (Yam) Family

Leaves of Wild Yam resemble those of *Smilax* (pages 238, 239), both vines being monocots. The term "yam" is often applied to certain sweet potatoes, but sweet potatoes are dicots, in the Morning Glory Family. There are some species of true yams that are grown in tropical climates for an edible tuber.

These Wild Yams are temperate climate plants that thrive in moist habitats. Note the thread-like flower clusters and the resulting 3-winged fruits.

Leaves of Hops are 3 to 5 lobed on long, twining vines. Some taxonomists have classified Hops and Hemp (*Canabis*) in the *Moraceae* (Mulberry) Family.

Hops
Humulus lupulus
Canabinaceae (Hemp) Family

Hops are dioecious plants with male (staminate) flowers in a branched panicle (left). Female flowers (pistillate) are in short spikes with overlapping bracts which resemble leafy cones (right).

Hops are cultivated for the "cones" which are used as flavoring for beer.

They have escaped cultivation, naturalized and thrive in moist, open areas.

Hog Peanut
Amphicarpa bracteata
Fabaceae (Pea or Legume) Family

These vines of deep, wooded areas produce two kinds of flowers. Pictured here are the loose clusters of pale lavender flowers that develop into 3-seeded pods. Another flower type at the base of the stem (not pictured) is usually without petals and its pod develops with only one seed. This pod, like the peanut of commerce, may become buried underground.

Hog peanut vines are weak and use other plants for support. At right, the vine is tangled with a woodland Aster.

247

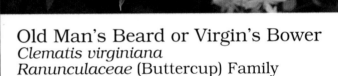

Old Man's Beard or Virgin's Bower
Clematis virginiana
Ranunculaceae (Buttercup) Family

Although they have similarities, *Clematis virginiana* is distinctly different from the Purple Virgin's Bower (page 240). *C. virginiana* blooms much later in the season.

This species has smaller flowers, each with 4 white sepals but no petals. In the fall, grayish-white, feathery seed heads look "beard-like."

Tag Alder
Alnus rugosa
Betulaceae (Birch) Family

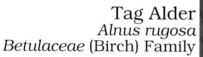

One of the first signs of spring is the appearance of Alder catkins before leaves appear on the trees and herbaceous plants begin to poke up through the forest floor.

Pendulous catkins (upper photos) are staminate (male) flowers. Pistillate (female) catkins are stubby (note arrow in upper left photo) and produce the cone-like fruits seen in the photo (lower left).

V. angustifoium is one of several species of blueberries which produce delicious fruit.

Early white, bell-shaped, flowers are borne in small clusters. By summer, juicy, blue berries are ready for picking and become a sweet treat for bears, birds and people.

This species grows from 1 to 2 feet high. Its shiny leaves are green on both surfaces.

Blueberry
Vaccinium angustifolium
Ericaceae (Heath) Family

Dewberry or Dwarf Raspberry
Rubus pubescens
Rosaceae (Rose) Family

Each spring, low-growing woody stems on the forest floor produce short herbaceous shoots up to 6 inches tall. White flowers give way to a cluster of fruit that looks like a red raspberry.

Because the fruit clings to its receptacle like a blackberry and does not pull away cleanly, it is technically a "dewberry." Some references name it Dwarf Raspberry.

June Berry, Serviceberry, Shadberry or Saskatoon Berry
Amelanchier spp.
Rosaceae (Rose) Family

Several species of *Amelanchier* are so similar they can be distinguished only by technical observations. Some references list up to 15 species. Common names given above will apply to all of this group.

Irregularly shaped white flower petals, as shown above, are a good representation. Appearance of flowers, slightly before the leaves fully expand, is typical growth pattern.

Pea-size fruits develop, first green, then turning reddish, finally becoming deep purple in color. These ripened fruits have a pleasant, sweet flavor.

Chokecherry
Prunus virginiana
Rosaceae (Rose) Family

With dark green leaves, dense, elongated flower heads appear on chokecherry branches in early spring. Later, nearly black fruits develop which are astringent to taste as fresh fruit, but are delicious when made into jelly or pancake syrup!

Pin Cherry
Prunus pensylvanica
Rosaceae (Rose) Family

Pin Cherry flowers appear as a "ready-made" corsage on the leafy branches of this small tree. Shiny red fruits develop mid-summer. These fruits are sour to taste but make excellent jelly.

Fly Honeysuckle plants are small shrubs about 3 feet in height. Greenish-white flowers come in pairs and produce unique sets of red berries. Ripened berries don't last long as they are relished by birds.

A later blooming Honeysuckle (*Diervilla lonicera*, Northern Bush Honeysuckle) is pictured on page 265.

Fly Honeysuckle
Lonicera canadensis
Caprifoliaceae (Honeysuckle) Family

Bunchberry or Dwarf Dogwood
Cornus canadensis
Cornaceae (Dogwood) Family

Being in the Dogwood Family and having a woody rhizome, Bunchberry is shown here rather than in the herbaceous plant section. Flowers are typically Dogwood with 4 showy white bracts surrounding a cluster of tiny greenish white flowers. By mid-summer a "bunch" of bright red berries develops.

Pointed, egg-shaped leaves on this plant are limited to a single whorl of 6 on a stem about 4 to 6 inches high.

Moist, but not wet, nutrient-rich woodlands are prime habitat for Bunchberry.

Labrador Tea
Ledum groenlandicum
Ericaceae (Heath) Family

Labrador Tea are small shrubs which grow in cold bogs. They brighten the landscape in spring with a flush of white 5-petaled blossoms.

Leaves, typically rolled on the edges, have a brownish wool on the underside.

Capsules develop that have a prominent beak (photo below).

Pale or Swamp Laurel
Kalmia polifolia
Ericaceae (Heath) Family

Thriving in a cold bog along with white flow-ering Labrador Tea, Swamp Laurel highlights the scene with color. Narrow, elliptical, leath-ery leaves have edges rolled downward. Being a shrubby plant, it stands about 2 feet high. Red fruits become brown at maturation.

258

Beach Plum is at home on sandy dunes and beaches of the Great Lakes. A shrubby plant, it may grow as much as 8 feet tall. Its branches become profusely covered with white blossoms in spring followed by marble-size, deep purple fruits.

These fruits will "pucker" your mouth when eaten fresh, but are fine made into jelly.

Beach Plum
Prunus maritima
Rosaceae (Rose) Family

Bearberry
Arctostaphylos uva-ursi
Ericaceae (Heath) Family

Bearberry is a sprawling plant of short upright shoots on a trailing woody stem. Leaves are leathery and evergreen. Tiny vase-shaped flowers hang in clusters. Red berries develop by mid-summer and unless eaten, remain through the winter.

Highbush Cranberry
Viburnum trilobum
Caprifoliaceae (Honeysuckle) Family

Highbush Cranberry has no relationship to the "Thanksgiving" cranberry which is in the Heath Family. Highbush is a large shrub 3 to 9 feet tall.

Large sterile (without stamen or pistil) flowers form a ring surrounding smaller, fertile, fruit-producing flowers in the center of the inflorescence. Pea-size fruits, which ripen in summer, are sour to taste but delicious as jelly or syrup.

V. trilobum along with several other *Viburnum* species are useful landscape shrubs.

Shrubby Cinquefoil
Potentilla fruticosa
Rosaceae (Rose Family

This native shrub is one of the most versatile plants in the country. It thrives on this rocky ledge along Lake Superior, but it has also become a mainstay of landscape planting in home gardens and commercial developments. In adverse conditions like the rocky crevice, it may get only 1 foot high, but in good soil, this shrub will reach 4 feet in height.

Wild Rose
Rosa spp.
Rosaceae (Rose) Family

Several species of native wild roses, in a variety of habitats, are abundant in this region. Species differences are subtle, such as the size and shape of the pointed, dried sepals on the hips (fruits) shown above. The sepals in the top photo all point outward but in the lower photo the sepals flatten in a star-like pattern. Another species difference is in number, size shape and location of prickles or thorns along the stem, while others have smooth stems.

Most have flowers that are variations of pink but white or yellow also occur. Flowers range in size less than 1 inch to over 3 inches across. All have compound leaves, but leaflet number varies from 3 to 11 from species to species.

Mountain Ash
Sorbus or Pyrus americana
Rosaceae (Rose) Family

Taxonomists differ in classifying Mountain Ash. Some place it in its own genus, *Sorbus*, while others combine it with *Pyrus*, the genus of Pears.

Another Mountain Ash, *S. decora* (not shown), is almost identical but has larger fruit and slightly shorter leaflets.

Native species, by whatever name, Mountain Ash trees are a lovely sight with white flower clusters in spring and masses of red-orange berries mid-summer through fall.

Northern Bush Honeysuckle
Diervilla lonicera
Caprifoliaceae (Honeysuckle) Family

Clusters of 2 to 6 funnel-shaped yellow flowers are usually located at the branch tips of Northern Bush Honeysuckle. Unlike other honeysuckles, it has leaves with serrated margins. This bushy shrub reaches 1 to 4 feet in height.

Ribes is the genus of Gooseberries and Currants, another group of similar species throughout this region. Basically, gooseberries have prickles on their stems. In contrast, currant stems are usually smooth.

Prickly Gooseberry is a small shrub growing about 3 feet tall. Its flowers have 5 fused petals forming a bell-like center surrounded by 5 greenish-white sepals.

Prickly Gooseberry
Ribes cynosbati
Saxifragaceae (Saxifrage) Family

Skunk Currant
Ribes glandulosum
Saxifragaceae
(Saxifrage) Family

Skunk Currant flowers are small in comparison to Prickly Gooseberry, and its 5 petals are distinctly separate.

What's in a name? This Currant has a distinct odor: The leaves smell like "skunk" when bruised and the fruits are so bad tasting, birds avoid them.

Small Cranberry
Vaccinium oxycoccus
Ericaceae (Heath) Family

A miniature version of Large Cranberry *(V. macrocarpon*, the "Thanksgiving" cranberry), Small Cranberry inhabits wet Sphagnum Moss bogs. Dainty flowers rise up just a few inches from trailing stems.

The yellow arrow above points to a cinnamon-colored spore capsule of Sphagnum Moss.

Red-osier Dogwood
Cornus stolonifera
Cornaceae (Dogwood) Family

Red-osier Dogwood spreads by stolons, forming dense thickets up to 8 feet or more. Young stems are reddish in color.

Clusters of white, 4-petaled flowers are flat-topped, about 2 inches across. Ripened berries resemble White Baneberry fruits (page 28).

This plant, along with other Dogwood species, is often used in landscaping as an ornamental shrub.

Ninebark
Physocarpus opulifolius
Rosaceae (Rose) Family

A large shrub up to 9 feet in height, Ninebark gives a showy display of rosy-pink buds before opening to white or pinkish flowers. Many stamens give a soft brush-like appearance to the open flowers.

Stems have bark that splits and peals off in strips with age and weathering.

Ninebark has become commercially available for landscape use.

Thimbleberry or Flowering Raspberry
Rubus parviflorus
Rosaceae (Rose) Family

What these raspberries lack in succulent, sweet flavor, they make up in a spring display of showy white flowers. Fruits, quite edible when ripe, taste more tart than common red raspberries. Large leaves, up to 8 inches across, have likeness to Maple leaves. Stems are without thorns and grow 3 to 6 feet high.

Meadowsweet
Spirea alba
Rosaceae (Rose) Family

White to pinkish flowers on a branched, spiraling inflorescence give Meadowsweet a distinctive look. Numerous protruding stamens make the flowers appear "woolly."

Stems are brownish and grow 2 to 6 feet high. Lance-shaped leaves are sharply toothed.

S. latifolia, a similar Meadowsweet, has wider, more coarsely-toothed leaves on a reddish to purple-brown stem. It is more common in the eastern part of the region, while *S. alba* is more prevalent in the western Great Lakes area.

Meadowsweet

Swamp Dewberry
Rubus spp.
Rosaceae (Rose) Family

Growing on peat land, this Dewberry is well-dressed in springtime with sparkling white flowers. It is a short, sprawling shrub standing only 1 to 2 feet high. Ripened fruit are purple-to-black by the end of summer.

Blackberry
Rubus Spp.
Rosaceae (Rose) Family

Blackberry thickets thrive in the forests of the Great Lakes region. There are several species, most of which can be recognized by white flowers, rambling, prickly canes and delicious purple-black berries that ripen by late summer.

Red-berried Elder
Sambucus pubens
Caprifoliaceae (Honeysuckle) Family

Red-berried Elder stands out in woodlands when large panicle-like bunches of red fruits command attention. These shrubs grow to 9 feet tall in moist woods.

Snowberry
Symphoricarpos albus
Caprifoliaceae (Honeysuckle) Family

Snowberry, an upright shrub to 3 feet high, becomes showy in late summer when clusters of white berries decorate the branches.

Red Maple
Acer rubrum
Aceraceae (Maple) Family

Red Maples show their true colors early in the season. Spring flowers are inconspicuous, but the red seeds in autumn take center stage.

Beaked Hazel
Corylus cornuta
Betulaceae (Birch) Family

Curious Beaked Hazel fruits have sticky, fuzzy husks containing a round "filbert" or Hazelnut.

Ripened Hazelnuts are soon harvested and stored away by hungry squirrels.

Grasses and Sedges

Sedges are sometimes described as "grass-like." Although they have similarities, these plants are in separate Families. Sedges are in the *Cyperaceae* Family. Grasses belong to *Poaceae (also called Graminae).* The two families, because of their similarities, belong to a higher level of classification (Order) called *Poales.* Common characteristics of *Poales* include blade-like leaves and flowers without petals or sepals.

Grasses have jointed, circular, and usually hollow stems. Most grasses prefer drier habitats.

Sedges have triangular, solid stems that are not jointed and normally thrive in wet places.

Cotton Grass
Eriophorum spp.
Cyperaceae (Sedge) Family

Soft, thread-like hairs mimicking cotton bolls at harvest in the South, cover the seed head of this sedge in the summer. This Cotton Grass grows in a bog environment.

Carex Sedge
Carex comosa
Cyperaceae (Sedge) Family

Carex species are monoecious, like corn, having pollen-forming flowers in tassels while seed forming flowers are in "ears." *Carex* pollen develops in a brown spike (see arrows). Seeds ripen in the inflated, pointed green flowers.

Carex Sedge
Carex intumescens
Cyperaceae (Sedge) Family

Bulrush species are many and hard to identify. This group thrives in wet places, even in standing water of ponds and lake shores. Some have leaves that closely resemble grasses and others look more like reeds.

Bulrush
Scirpus spp.
Cyperaceae (Sedge) Family

Hard Stem Bulrush
Scirpus acutus
Cyperaceae (Sedge) Family

Wild or Foxtail Barley
Hordeum jubatum
Poaceae (Grass) Family

Wild Barley is a perennial grass in the same genus as the
barley of commerce. Many road sides become lined with
the soft, purplish-green "foxtail" seed heads in summer. It
also thrives in meadows and waste places.

Timothy
Phleum pratense
Poaceae (Grass) Family

Timothy, named Meadow Cat's Tail elsewhere, is a perennial found growing in meadows and road ditches. Like a small bottle brush, the cylindrical, green flower head has a unique appearance. It has been cultivated for use as a pasture and hay crop.

Smooth Brome Grass
Bromis inermis
Poaceae (Grass) Family

These flowers of *B. inermis* hang in loose panicles. Dry, open meadows and road sides are common habitat where this grass has become naturalized. Smooth Brome Grass, brought from Europe, is cultivated extensively for pasture and hay.

Common to wet, meadow-like areas, Reed Canary Grass grows aggressively once established. This native grass is coarse stemmed and tall (up to 6 feet).

"Ribbon Grass" and "Gardener's Garters" are names given to variations that have white stripes running the length of the leaves. These grasses make handsome landscape plants, especially in areas where their invasive tendencies will not become a problem.

Reed Canary Grass
Phalaris arundinacea
Poaceae (Grass) Family

Ferns, Clubmosses and Horsetails

What's not blooming? Ferns, Clubmosses and Horsetails are plants without flowers and seeds, but they also have their place in the "wild" world. They are set apart because their sexual reproductive cycle is completed without the formation of a seed. Visible reproductive structures of these plants produce spores on the underside of leaves (fronds) in Ferns or in "cones" at the tip of a stalk as with Horsetails and Clubmosses. These spores continue the reproductive process, forming an inconspicuous intermediate generation which then completes the life cycle of these unique plants.

Northern Maidenhair Fern with Large-flowered Trillium
Adiantum pedatum
Polypodiaceae (Polypody) Family

Lacy fronds of Maidenhair Fern make an attractive accompaniment to Trillium blossoms. These delicate-looking fronds form a fan-shaped pattern which makes them easy to recognize. Height may vary from 12 to 18 inches. Like most ferns, *A. pedatum* keeps good form from spring to fall.

Forest Horsetail
Equisetum sylvaticum
Equisetaceae (Horsetail) Family

Forest Horsetail is a "bushy" horsetail with whorls of branches spreading outward from joints in the stem. The "fertile" stems in the photo have spore cones at the tips. Sterile stems (not shown) do not have cones and their whorls branch 2 or 3 times, creating a plume-like appearance. Other *Equisetum* species, lacking whorls of branches, are called Scouring Rush because their stems are rough with silica and feel like sandpaper.

Running Clubmoss is evergreen with horizontal stems creeping over the surface of the ground. Upright stems branch, supporting "cones" at the tips.

Running or Staghorn Clubmoss
Lycopodium clavatum
Lycopodiaceae (Clubmoss) Family

Fern Fiddleheads

"Variations on a Theme"

Cinnamon Fern
Osmunda cinnamomea
Osmundaceae (Royal Fern) Family

Cinnamon Ferns have two types of fronds. Narrow, erect fertile fronds begin green, but soon wither and turn to a cinnamon-brown as the spores form. Sterile fronds are wider and longer (up to 3 feet long), arching outward and remain green through the summer.

Fern Fiddleheads

Fiddleheads are the beginning of fern leaves called fronds. Fronds begin to grow on underground stems (rhizomes). They poke through the soil, coiled like the scroll of a fiddle and come in many shapes and sizes depending on species.

289

Sensitive Fern
Onoclea sensibilis
Polypodiaceae (Polypody) Family

Sensitive to cold, green fronds of this fern rapidly turn brown with the first frost of autumn. Sterile fronds with large leaflets are the most prominent, being 2 feet tall. Brownish fertile fronds are about 1 foot tall. These ferns grow in a wide range of habitats, from full sun to shade and wet to dry soils.

Spore Producing Leaflets

Interrupted Fern
Osmunda claytoniana
Osmundaceae (Royal Fern) Family

Fertile fronds, also the tallest fronds, stand upright in *O. claytoniana*. Spore-producing leaflets are located only on the central part of the frond, "interrupting" the pattern of green sterile leaflets. Sterile fronds without brown leaflets are shorter and bend outward. These ferns thrive in shaded woodlands as well as full sun environments.

Rattlesnake Fern
Botrychium virginianum
Ophioglossaceae (Adder's-tongue) Family

Rattlesnake Fern is an oddity because it has one
12 inch stalk which divides into two fronds. A lacy,
green, sterile frond spreads out like a fan. The other
is a fertile frond that projects upward. Once the fertile frond produces spores, it withers and disappears.
Moist, shaded woodlands are home to this species.

Bracken Fern
Pteridium aquilinum
Polypodiaceae (Polypody) Family

One of the most common ferns, Bracken Ferns are invasive and form large colonies in open sunny areas or in light shade. Fronds grow 3 feet tall.

Spores are produced in lines on the underside of the leaflets.

Rock or Common Polypody Fern
Polypodium virginianum
Polypodiaceae (Polypody) Family

Rock Polypody Ferns are evergreen, even in harsh
northern winters. As the name implies, crevices in rocks
are a favorite habitat. Rusty-colored sporangia appear
on the under side of the fronds, ready to disperse their
spores to start a new generation of ferns.

British Soldiers

British Soldiers, *Cladonia cristatella*, are Lichens. Lichens are a combination of two organisms, algae and fungi, growing together. Algae are green, containing chlorophyll, allowing photosynthesis for sugar (food) production. Fungi do not have chlorophyll, but feed from the algae. In turn, the fungi provides minerals and a moist environment for the algae. Red tops are reproductive structures which appear in springtime.

PLANT FAMILY FACTS
A Few Common Traits

Flower structure is a major determining factor for sorting plants into families. Structure of the flower 1) includes counting parts in each whorl, such as the number of sepals, petals, stamens and carpels; and 2) notes in detail the position of these parts, one to another, such as fusing of petals to form a bell. Leaf arrangement, stem characteristics and even root structure aid in placement of plants into categories.

Plant identification is a fascinating study. For readers interested in learning more about recognizing and grouping plants into families, we recommend *Taxonomy of Flowering Plants* by Porter or *Manual of Vascular Plants of Northeastern United States and Adjacent Canada* by Gleason and Cronquist.

Botanical names are governed by the International Code of Botanical Nomenclature. Family names are usually recognized by the suffix *aceae* attached to the stem of one genus name within the family. There are eight family names of Angiosperms that were historically given an *ae* ending. Traditionally they are still used. In this guide, both the International Code Rule and traditional name are listed.

ANGIOSPERMS

ANGIOSPERM is the term given to all **flowering, seed producing plants**. This category is divided again into two groups: MONOCOTS and DICOTS. *Monocots* have 1 cotyledon (embryonic leaf) in their seeds, flower parts in 3's or multiples of 3 and blade-like leaves with parallel veins. *Dicots* have 2 cotyledons, flower parts usually in 4's or 5's. Leaves show a netted vein pattern.

MONOCOTS

Alismataceae (Arrowhead)
Wetland herbaceous plants with arrow-, lance- or oval-shaped leaves. Flower parts in whorls of 3. Petals usually white.

Amaryllidaceae (Amaryllis)
Similar to Liliaceae except the sepals and petals are attached above the ovary (epigynous) rather than below (hypogynous).

Araceae (Arum or Calla)
Flowers bloom atop a spike-like structure called a spadix, surrounded by a leaf-like spathe. Tropical genera in this family include *Philodendron*, *Anthurium* and *Monstera* (Split-leaf Philodendron) and are grown as houseplants.

Cyperaceae (Sedge)
Herbaceous plants resembling grasses, but stems are not jointed and are usually triangular in cross section. Flowers lack petals but may have bristles or hairs instead. A bract called a glume or scale covers the flower.

Dioscoreaceae (Yam)
Flowers have 3 sepals and 3 petals which look alike (tepals) and 6 stamens. Vining plants, Yams have heart-shaped leaves growing up from thick rhizomes or tubers. Most Yams are tropical, but *Dioscorea villosa* is native to this region. Red, orange or yellow "yams" marketed in grocery stores are really "*sweet potatoes*", members of *Convolvulaceae* (Morning Glory Family).

Iridaceae (Iris)
Rhizome or corm producing. Parallel-veined leaves fold lengthwise around the stem at their base. Flower parts in whorls of 3.

Liliaceae (Lily)
Parallel veined leaves. Flower parts in multiples of 3. Sepals often colored and shaped like petals. Petals usually bell-shaped. Plants often form bulbs.

Orchidaceae (Orchid)

Flower parts in whorls of 3. Sepals often petaloid (petal-like). Two lateral petals with a larger third petal forming a pouch, sac or lip-like structure. Leaves parallel-veined. Orchid species are found from arctic to tropical regions. Most temperate region Orchids are terrestrial (grow in soil). Tropical species tend to be epiphytic (growing on tree branches and taking nourishment from the air and water).

Poaceae or Gramineae (Grass)

Mostly herbaceous plants with jointed stems, usually hollow between the joints. Flowers lack sepals and petals. 3 or 6 stamens and a pistil are between two scales called the lemma and palea. Other bracts called glumes may surround the flower. Fruit in grasses is a grain where the ovary wall is fused to the seed coat, like a corn kernel. Some of the largest grasses include corn and bamboo.

Typhaceae (Cattail)

Wetland herbaceous plants with ridged stems and long, blade-like leaves. Tiny male and female flowers bloom separately on a spike at the stem tip.

DICOTS

Aceraceae (Maple)

Trees or shrubs with opposite leaves. Usually small flowers. Fruits are "winged" samaras.

Anacardiaceae (Sumac or Cashew)

Mostly tropical trees and shrubs. Cashew, Mango and Pistachio trees are widely known for their delicious fruits. Our temperate climate Sumac, Poison Ivy and Poison Oak are in this family. Both temperate and tropical family members have toxic parts. Structures of reproductive parts in flowers put all these plants in the same family group.

Apiaceae or Umbelliferae (Parsley)

Inflorescence usually a flat-topped umbel. Often referred to as Carrot, Celery, Dill, or Parsnip Family.

Apocynaceae (Dogbane)

Herbaceous or woody plants. Flower parts in whorls of 5. Petals fused to form a bell shape. Stems have a milky juice. Several tropical species including Plumeria and Oleander are well known. Several species are toxic.

Araliaceace (Ginseng)

Small flowers usually bloom in a round umbel. Compound leaves either alternate or in 3's.

Aristolochiaceae (Birthwort)

Although most in this family are tropical, Wild Ginger is not. Flowers have 3 purple-brown, petal-like sepals flaring out like a cup. Leaves are heart-shaped. Dutchman's Pipe is another example of this family.

Asclepiadaceae (Milkweed)

Five-part flower whorls with the sepals and petals curving backwards. Another set of appendages arise from the petals or the stamens, forming a petal-like "corona." Stems have a milky juice.

Asteraceae or Compositae (Aster)

Often called Sunflower or Daisy Family, this is the largest family of plants numbering thousands of species in a broad range of habitats. Porter reports about 950 genera and 20,000 species. The largest genus, Senecio, has about 2,300 species alone. Many small flowers, in dense heads, appear as one flower like Asters and Sunflowers. This dense flower formation is the key structural characteristic. Often a ring of ray flowers with showy petals surrounds a central disk of minute, seed-producing, disk flowers. Others have only disk flowers or only ray flowers.

Balsaminaceae (Touch-me-not)

Succulent stems, thin leaves and irregular-shaped flowers. Most are tropical, such as the Impatiens used as annual bedding plants. Ripe seedpods coil and spring open when touched, forcefully ejecting their seeds.

Berberidaceae (Barberry)

Mostly woody shrubs but there are 3 herbaceous genera in our area, Podophyllum (May Apple), Jeffersonia (Twinleaf), and Caulophyllum (Blue Cohosh). Flower parts in 4 or 6.

Betulaceae (Birch)

A family of trees and shrubs. Flowers are usually in the form of catkins (pendulous spikes of diminutive flowers) which bear only male or female flowers.

Boraginaceae (Borage)

Mostly bristly, hairy, herbaceous plants. Five fused petals form a tube on which the stamens are attached. Inflorescence usually coiled, unrolling as it grows.

Brassicaceae or Cruciferae (Mustard)

Flowers with 4 petals and normally 6 stamens. Ovary 2-celled, forming a long, narrow, pod-like fruit (silique).

Campanulaceae (Bluebell)

Flower parts in 5's. Petals fused in the form of a bell. Stamens normally free standing.

Cannabinaceae (Hemp)

Plants are herbaceous, either vining or erect. Male and female flowers are usually on separate plants. Female flowers are without petals and in bract-like spikes. Male flowers are in panicles, each flower having 5 sepals and 5 stamens. Only 2 genera, Cannabis (Hemp) and Humulus (Hops) are in this family. Some taxonomists place them in Moraceae (Mulberry Family) and others in Urticaceae (Nettle Family).

Caprifoliaceae (Honeysuckle)

Most are woody shrubs or vines. Flowers with 5 parts per whorl. Petals are fused, with stamens attached to the petals. Twinflower is an exception to the woody characteristic of the family.

Caryophyllaceae (Pink)

Flowers usually have notched petals, some looking like they have been cut with "pinking" shears, hence their name "Pink." Pinks come in many colors. Flower parts in whorls of 5 (sometimes 4). Stems have swollen joints.

Cistaceae (Rockrose)

Low-growing plants with crowded, scale-like leaves. Flowers have 5 petals which age and fall quickly. Many stamens.

Convolvulaceae (Morning-glory)

Herbaceous plants, many with vining growth habit. Tubular or funnel-shaped flowers with 5 fused petals. Genus Cuscuta (Dodder) is a parasitic weed.

Cornaceae (Dogwood)

Mostly trees and shrubs with the exception of Bunchberry. Small flowers have parts in 4's. Inflorescence may be surrounded by showy bracts as in Flowering Dogwood or Bunchberry.

Droseraceae (Sundew)

Small, insectivorous plants of bogs. Leaves are spoon-shaped in a rosette. Flowers on a slender stalk have 5 petals.

Ericaceae (Heath)

Flower parts in 4's or 5's. Petals often fused to form a bell shape. Mostly woody shrubs, but also low-growing forms such as Bearberry.

Fabaceae or Leguminosae (Pea or Legume)

Another large family. Flowers are irregular (will divide into mirror images only if cut in one direction). Five petals with 2 fused enclosing the pistil; 2 form "wings" to the sides and one forms a larger "banner" over the top of the flower. Fruit is a legume or pod.

Fumariaceae (Fumitory)

See Papaveraceae.

Gentianaceae (Gentian)

Flower parts in 4's or 5's with petals fused together and stamens attached to the corolla (fused whorl of petals).

Geraniaceae (Geranium)

Flower parts in whorls of 5. Pistil has a beak-like structure called a "cranes bill" which splits away into 5 curled strips, each containing 1 or 2 seeds.

Hydrophyllaceae (Waterleaf)

Flower parts in 5's. Petals fused into a bell shape. Stamens often long and extend beyond the edge of the petals. Leaves often have spots which look like "water spots."

Hypericaceae (St. Johns'-wort)
Herbaceous or shrubby plants. Leaves often with dots. Yellow flowers. Flower parts in 3's or 5's.

Lamiaceae or Labiatae (Mint)
Aromatic herbaceous plants. Stems square. Small flowers with 5 petals irregular in shape. Two long and 2 short stamens; a fifth stamen either absent or smaller and infertile.

Lentibulariaceae (Bladderwort)
Mostly insectivorous water plants. Submerged leaves have "bladders" which trap small aquatic animals for a source of nutrients. Flowers have 2 "lips" nearly the same as Scrophulariaceae.

Lythraceae (Loosestrife)
Flowers with 3 to 6 petals are often purple, in terminal clusters. Narrow, upright growth pattern. (Different from yellow-flowered Loosestrife plants, members of the Primrose Family.)

Malvaceae (Mallow)
Flower parts in multiples of 5. Stamens cluster around the pistil as in Hibiscus and Hollyhocks.

Nymphaeaceae (Water Lily)
Plants root in mud at the bottom of shallow lakes and ponds. Flower stalks arise from the base of the plants. Leaves float flat on the water surface.

Onagraceae (Evening Primrose)
Flower parts in whorls of 4 (some in 2's). Seeds often have tufts of hairs allowing wind dispersal.

Oxalidaceae Wood Sorrel)
Juice of the plant is sour, containing oxalic acid. Compound leaves have 3 heart-shaped leaflets. Flower parts in whorls of 5.

Papaveraceae (Poppy)
Milky juice in stem. Flower parts in multiples of 4. Numerous stamens. Lobed leaves. Corydalis and Dicentra, included in this family, are placed in Fumeriaceae by some taxonomists.

Plantaginaceae (Plantain)
Non-showy flowers on a slender stalk arising from the crown of the plant. Leaves in a basal rosette.

Polemoniaceae (Phlox)
Flower parts in 5's. Fused petals form a tube. Stamens partially fused to the petals (corolla).

Polygalaceae (Milkwort)
Flower parts irregular, like legumes. One example illustrated here is Polygala.

Polygonaceae (Buckwheat)
Stems with swollen joints. Tiny flowers are without petals and clustered on a spike-like stem tip. Sepals may be colored.

Portulacaceae (Purslane)
Flowers with 2 sepals and usually 5 petals. Leaves tend to be thick and succulent. An exception, Spring Beauty, has thin leaves.

Primulaceae (Primrose)
Flower parts in whorls of 5. Stamens attached to the center of petals. Evening Primrose plants are in the Onagraceae (Evening Primrose) Family, not in the Primrose Family. Confusing?

Pyrolaceae (Pyrola or Wintergreen)
Small, basically evergreen, woodland plants. Flower parts in whorls of 5. Some taxonomists consider this a subfamily of Ericaceae (Heath Family).

Ranunculaceae (Buttercup or Crowfoot)
Flower parts highly variable in number. Three to many sepals that may be petal-like. Certain species lack petals. Commonly many stamens and pistils form a "button" in the flower center.

Rosaceae (Rose)
Flower parts in multiples of 5. Numerous stamens. A large family including most of the temperate climate fruits such as apples, pears, peaches, plums, raspberries, and strawberries.

Rubiaceae (Madder or Bedstraw)
Mostly tree or shrubs (including Coffee and Gardenia) in tropical regions. In this temperate climate, there are small herbaceous species. Flower parts usually in whorls of 4. Petals fused with stamens attached.

Santalaceae (Sandalwood)
A group of parasitic plants that attach to other species to draw nourishment, especially early in their development. Flowers have 5 sepals, no petals and 5 stamens. Mostly tropical.

Sarraceniaceae (Pitcher Plant)
Insectivorous plants with tubular leaves that collect water and insects. Flower stalks arise from the base of the plants. Flower parts in whorls of 5. Style on pistil forms an umbrella shape.

Saxifragaceae (Saxifrage)
Flowers resemble those of the Rose Family. Leaves usually form a rosette. Flower parts in 4's or 5's

Scrophulariaceae (Snapdragon or Figwort)
Flower parts in whorls of 5. Unequal petals fused into a tube often with lobes forming an upper and lower "lip." Five stamens fused to petals, usually 4 fertile and 1 sterile.

Solanaceae (Tomato or Nightshade)
Also known as Potato or Tobacco Family. Mostly herbaceous, but occasionally woody. Some are vines such as Bittersweet Nightshade. Flower parts in 5's. Stamens attached to fused petals. Several species have toxic substances.

Urticaceae (Nettle)
Often have stinging hairs on stems and leaves. Flowers are inconspicuous on string-like racemes coming from leaf axils.

Valerianaceae (Valerian)
Fused petals form a tube with 5 flaring tips. Stamens and pistil extend beyond the flaring petal tips. A single pistil forms one dry fruit with the dried sepals (called the pappus) remaining attached.

Verbenaceae (Vervain)
Small, 4- or 5-part flowers in spikes or heads. Fused petals with 2 pairs of stamens attached.

Violaceae (Violet)
Flowers with 5 petals, a lower wide petal often extends back into a spur. Low growing herbaceous plants.

PTERIDOPHYTES
Non-flowering Vascular Plants
Ferns, Clubmosses and Horsetails

These plants have vessels (xylem and phloem) which conduct water and nutrients throughout the plant. The mode of reproduction differs because these plants do not produce fruit and seeds from flowers. Pteridophytes have spore-forming structures called sporangia; from these spores, a new plant life-cycle begins.

Equisetaceae (Horsetail)
Sporangia are located on top of ribbed, jointed stems. Non-green remnants of leaves form at the joints. Green stems carry out photosynthesis to nourish the plants. Curiously, the ribs take up silica, making them rough.

Lycopodiaceae (Clubmoss)
Mostly trailing plants. Upright branches have small, green leaves. Sporangia are found on special leaves at branch tips.

Ophioglossaceae (Succulent Ferns)
Ferns with soft, fleshy stems that have 1 (sometimes 2) leaves. Adder's-tongue, Grape and Rattlesnake Ferns are representative of this Family.

Osmundaceae (Flowering Ferns)
"Flowering" is a misnomer as no true flowers are formed. Rather, modified portions of fronds have spore cases which are conspicuous and may appear as withered flowers.

Polypodiaceae (Polypody Family)
Largest of the fern families, Polypody Ferns have spore cases on the underside of their fronds. These spores may be in dots over the surface or arranged along the margin of the fronds.

What's in a name? How do plants get their names? Some names are easier to figure out and study than others. For example, Polypody means "many feet." Fronds grow from the rhizome (underground stem). "Many feet" refer to the footprint-like scars left on the rhizome when the fronds age and break off.

Scientific Names

Common Names

Showy Lady's Slipper
Minnesota State Flower